Nice Girls Do

An expert in the field reveals her unique and
positive approach to complete fulfillment

Dr. Kassorla's techniques have been tested through
hundreds of men and women ranging in age from
twenty to sixty, including married couples, singles
and people living together. Her conclusion is that you
have an inalienable right to sexual fulfillment, and
that you inherited this right at birth.

SELECTED BY THE LITERARY GUILD

D0830195

Nice Girls Do

DR. IRENE KASSORLA

PLAYBOY
PAPERBACKS

TO MY FATHER

Who taught me the meaning of tenderness with his soft cheeks and gentle hands.

Contents

Case
Histories

Acknowledgments

While it required both a psychologist and a woman who has been able to experiment with her own sensuality to write this book, it also required many loving friends and associates to stand behind her during three and a half years of writing and rewriting, offering their priceless help and support.

My thanks go to my loyal and hardy assistants, Karen Philipp, June Berk, Linda Block, Amy Honbo, Barbara Kadish and Helen Antler, for their tender, loving care. These women often wore emotional roller skates to handle the flood of manuscript pages which met them every morning.

With gratitude and respect I send bouquets to Ellen Shahan, the brilliant editor whose skill finalized the fifth and last writing of the book; Auriel Douglas, who was willing to start at 5 a.m. with me each morning, rewriting and pulling together endless piles of research, case histories and other data which resulted in the fourth draft; Craig Buck for his prudent advice and help with rewriting and reorganization, and Bobbie Tropp for her skill with syntax and grammar, which together resulted in the third draft; Brett Howard, for pulling me up off the floor when I was discouraged and ready to quit and inspiring me to start all over again and create the second draft of the book; and Sheldon Kardener, my dear and beautiful psychiatrist, whose loving encouragement guided me into daring to experiment with the sensuous child inside of me so I could sit down and write the first draft of *Nice Girls Do*.

Behind every successful person I believe there's a smiling and approving mother. So my thanks and appreciation go to "Ma." My mother's name is Bertha, and we affectionately call her "Hasa Blooma" because she is so like a healthy and flourishing flower.

When I speak of love and support, my thoughts go immediately to my daughters, Ronnie and Jackie. How blessed I feel knowing them: lovely cameos of femininity and sensuality, dear and wonderful young women. A mother couldn't be prouder.

And now it's time to take my hand and enter into your sexual adventuring. Together we will share in the loving experience.

Take My Hand

Love and desire are the spirit's wings
to great deeds.

—GOETHE

You stand before your mirror—nude. In the soft glow of light you can see the contours of your reflection. Your body swells with expectation. Your flesh is rosy with excitement and warmth. You're full of anticipation as you fantasize how romantic and fulfilling sex will be.

You're in the mood.

You're ready for love . . . for that wild flight, body kindling body. You know that tonight will be the night.

Everything will be perfect.

Soon you'll be plunging into the passionate ride. It will be filled with turbulent, fleshy moments that stir a tempest in your heart. You're longing for the sensual storms, the thunder of the romantic electricity you've read about in novels and seen in films. You pray your fantasies will come true as you wait for your mate.

At last you're together in bed. You're so happy and

13

expectant as you begin to make love. Soon the hot juices will flow through you.

But nothing quite seems to work!

Your imagined ecstasies dissolve. You don't flow with the aura of your lovemaking. Instead you are grabbed by old fears. Invisible monitors hover over you as negative memories begin to play on your mind. Angers, guilts and inhibitions move into your bed. Your mood snaps, and you lose the joyful promise of sexual fulfillment.

In disgust you silently rationalize, "Sex, who needs it? It doesn't mean that much to me anyway. It never did!"

You feel lonely, disappointed and resentful.

> And the silence and the distance
> grow, because your lovemaking
> missed.

Then there are those times when both you and your partner feel affectionate. You start out on a delightful sexual high. And . . . you consummate the act.

But alas, this too misses! Either he ejaculates too soon, or you don't climax.

Again, you end up disappointed. You feel frustrated and inadequate. You think, "Expecting much more just isn't realistic."

You remind yourself about the law of compensation, sadly shake your head from side to side and sigh, "Nobody has everything!"

You cover up your feelings and lie to your partner. You assure him that the sex was just fine. Anyway it doesn't matter anymore. Now it's the companionship that counts.

"Everyone knows that once the honeymoon is over,

sex is all downhill," you say to yourself. "We've been together too long to be lovers."

> And the silence and the distance
> grow, because the lovemaking
> wasn't good.

Then there are other times when your body is with your partner, but your mind is off on "some enchanted island." You don't want to have sex. You don't even want to be touched. But you think you should oblige because you *owe* it to him.

> Besides, you're afraid to say no.

You don't want to hurt his feelings. So you go ahead and do it, hating every minute.

To sustain your excitement (in these not-so-loving encounters), you conjure up erotic fantasies about friends or strangers. Though you're sharing bodies in bed, your mind is light-years away.

> And the silence and the distance
> grow, because the lovemaking
> was obligatory.

Then there are those rare times when sex is life's wealth. You can hardly believe they happen. It's like a miracle, a languorous festival where you annihilate space and erase time. But you're not sure how you got there, and you're worried you'll never be able to get back. Maybe it's better if you don't, because some jealous god might strike you down for having so much pleasure.

You think to yourself, "Do I deserve all this joy? Could I get hurt by having so many good feelings? I don't want to be that dependent on someone else. I don't need that much closeness, that much intimacy. It scares me. It's all too good. And I'm afraid it won't last."

So even though it was perfect, you pull away. You do anything you can to separate: you *must* get up to find a cigarette; you just *have* to make that important phone call; or you feel *compelled* to argue about something you know is trivial.

Criticism and bickering take over. You feel upset and dissatisfied. You may hate it, but at least the separation and suffering are familiar. You know how to handle feeling angry and resentful, as . . .

> The silence and the distance
> grow, even after the lovemaking
> was perfect!

But your painful old patterns *can* stop. Those special, idyllic times don't have to be so rare.

YOU DESERVE SOMETHING BETTER.

You can get more from sex, from love, and from life. In this book you will learn a step-by-step process for achieving complete sexual gratification.* It's called the PLEASURE PROCESS.

Take My Hand

I want to invite you, the reader, to take my hand and come along with me on an adventure into the hidden mysteries of your extraordinary psyche and soma, your mind and your body.

---

* My techniques have been tested with over 500 men and women ranging in ages from 20 to 60. This sampling includes married couples, singles, and people living together, all of whom comprise a cross-cultural representation from the United States, Australia, Great Britain, France and Italy.

Part of our adventure together will take place in my office, where you can sit beside me as an invisible observer, a silent friend. You will be able to listen in on the therapy sessions that I conduct with my patients— work right along with us and share in what's happening.

Hearing my patients talk about their sexual problems and the important issues that are concerning women today will help you to identify and sort out the unknowns and unconscious misunderstandings of your sexual history. The solutions they work through will offer you guidelines and answers in solving your own problems.

As their progress unfolds, so will yours; as they become more insightful, feel more positive and fall in love with themselves and their sensuality, so will you. Become your own therapist, improving your own life; become a self-actualized woman.

Your Four-Year-Old Adviser

By the time you were four years old your adult sexual patterns and lifestyle were fixed. They were incorporated into your thinking by the myths and archaic notions about sex that you comprehended at that young age. Today, if I instructed you to let a four-year-old financial adviser take over your affairs, you would probably be very concerned. Yet, each of us is allowing a four-year-old sexual adviser who lives deep inside our unconscious to manage our sexual and sensual affairs today.

THIS ISN'T GOOD ENOUGH—OR SAFE
ENOUGH—FOR YOU.

You can start managing your *own* life now. You have the opportunity with your mature thinking to erase the old "forbidden tapes" (see pages 109 to 111) and design a new lifestyle and sexual pattern based on your adult preferences and desires. I don't want you to allow that small, frightened child buried deep within your past to make decisions about your sexual behavior today.

Is Sex Necessary?

James Thurber once asked the question, "Is sex necessary?" My immediate answer is an unqualified *yes*. Women are undergoing a sexual renaissance. After centuries of guilt and repression, the bait of sexual pleasure has at long last been separated from the hook of reproduction. We finally have acquired sexual freedom. Women now have the opportunity to experience their full sexual potential, however and whenever they wish. It is my purpose here to help women rid themselves of any remaining sexual shackles, and to help them do so with ease, dignity and pride.

For me, sex is a central force in life—an act of love, an act of godlike procreation, and an act of fun and recreation. For other writers and philosophers, sex is:

—Night without a morning! . . . the cloudless summer sun, Nature gay adorning;

—The strange bewilderment which overtakes one person on account of another person;

—Nature's second sun;

—Second life . . . warms every vein, and beats in every pulse;

—A credulous thing;

—A smoke raised with the fumes of sighs; madness most discreet;

—Where heart, and soul, and sense, in concert move, And the blood's lava, and the pulse a blaze, Each kiss a heart-quake.[1]

Freud marked history and changed scientific thinking when he dealt with the question of how necessary sex is. He wrote volumes arguing that the motivation for *all* human behavior was based on sex. I cannot support Freud's all-encompassing thesis on personality development. But while one could certainly argue that it is possible to survive without sex . . . or walks in the park, or music, or laughter, or the other sweet extras of living that are *not* primary biological needs . . .

WHY SHOULD YOU?

Our Inhibiting Pasts

Women have stayed at home and kept their sexuality underground and under control. The dictum has been transmitted from mother to daughter: "Get married, raise a family and please your husband. Forget about sex, passion and sensuality. Only nymphomaniacs are sexually indulgent. Men need a variety of sex partners and plenty of orgasms. Women only need their husbands."

Women have kept their sensuality in the closet or taken it on the sneak. When a woman did ache for intercourse or multiple orgasms (you know, those orgasms that "nice girls" shouldn't even be thinking about), there was always that secretive one-nighter or that occasional man waiting on the sidelines. In extramarital affairs women could allow themselves to be "sexy" and have fun. It is common for doctors like myself to hear confessions from women about torrid affairs with their husband's "best friend," but in their marriage, the door to their sensuality had to be *shut tight*.

It is a constant surprise to me to find otherwise knowledgeable women who still believe that "excesses" or "extremes" in sexual behavior will lead to dangerous consequences, such as loss of control, mental disorders, or irresponsible behavior. Such fears have been expressed to me by female patients in Europe, Canada, the United States and Australia. Their responses to these fears are usually very much the same. They turn off their sensual excitement as they are approaching orgasm because they are afraid that, if they continue on, they could "become epileptic," "lose control indefinitely," "have a heart attack," "burst a blood vessel," cause themselves "irreversible brain damage," or look ridiculous to their husbands as they pant and writhe.

Even the descriptive words commonly applied to sex suggest there is some kind of danger or loss of control associated with intercourse. For example, the Greek word *ekstasis*, from which our word *ecstasy* derives, connotes being beside oneself, deranged, beyond reason or self-control. The implication is always the same: there's something definitely wrong with heightened passion and sensual feelings.

Here is part of a case history from a patient whose concerns about her husband's judgments and behavior took priority over her sexual pleasure.

GWEN AND HER TERRORS

When Harry and I first start making love, I'm happy. I love him and want the closeness. I like the feelings we both get as the excitement begins. We both enjoy that part. Harry knows how to get me going. But when he does, the fast way I start moving my pelvis and hips frightens me. The lower part of my body goes into a fluttering, nervous kind of motion with such speed, it feels like there is a

*motor attached. I move so fast it's not human, it's
not me. I'm afraid Harry will start laughing at me
or that he'll lose his erection because all my shak-
ing sometimes dislodges his penis.*

*The whole thing isn't worth it. I feel so crazy. My
heart beats too fast and scares me. I think I could
go insane if I continue on much more. I'm afraid.
I don't want to go out of control or go insane.
Nothing is worth that. I'm not willing to risk it
when just being that close to Harry is so satisfying. So I cut it all off. I tell him I want to stop and
ask him to have his orgasm.*

Many women offer similar reports about how their
"cutting-off" phases occur. For some women it's hearing their own rapid breathing that causes them to halt;
others are too self-conscious to make even one audible
sound, and the fear that something "sexy" might slip
out forces them to stop; others want to be silly, laugh
and sing, and they're worried they'll appear inappropriate. They are so afraid that their partners will judge
them negatively, or think they sound ridiculous, that
they back away from their sexual climb.

Psychiatrist Dr. Therese Benedek describes the phenomenon this way:

Unconscious fear of ego regression may impede the
orgasmic capacity. . . . Since [a woman's] sexual experience is diffuse, this regression often feels to her as
a loss of herself. Many women experience this regression in the ego state—a psychological precursor to
orgasm—as an intolerable threat. Sometimes this is
described as a fear of becoming helpless, fear of being
completely at the mercy of uncontrollable impulses
and being unable to become oneself again.[2]

As the woman's preorgasmic excitement mobilizes, apprehension about these vague fears, losses, insanity, threats and anticipated punishments increases. "Psychologists Oswald Schwarz has called sex the only function that cannot lie. He means that while we may successfully hide behind facades and deceptions in other areas of our life, in sexual relations we reveal ourselves to our partner as we really are. And this can be a threatening thought to one who wishes to remain hidden."[3]

Many women fear that their most cherished ego ideal, their self-esteem, will collapse if they reveal themselves as sensual beings. No matter what sort of stimulation is applied, the anxiety of submitting to the growing sexual tension is greater than the anticipated joy culminating in the release of orgasm. As a protection against the experience of this anxiety, each woman makes up her own reasons and excuses as she stops herself and signals her partner to orgasm.

As a people, our culture has all but destroyed our desire and motivation to explore passionate loving, continuous orgasms, and joyous sensuality. Dr. Alexander Lowen notes that "a totality of response to any situation is unusual in our culture. We are all in too much conflict to surrender fully to any feeling."[4] Women have probably been hit the hardest by these pressures and taboos. Through the centuries they have been spoon-fed such worn-out stereotypes as:

—"All that men care about is your *body*."
—"If you give them what they want, they won't *respect* you."
—"Men will only *use* you."

There are women today who feel stuck in the dogmas of yesteryear. They live with the belief that if they dare to be sensual, they'll be flooded with feelings and the dam will burst.

> Women are trained to hide their sexual feelings. They are trained to be passive and wait for the man to make the first move toward sexual relations. An active woman, therefore, may feel a great deal of guilt because her action is not "normal"; and she may also be considered unfeminine.[5]

After all this negative propagandizing, it's no wonder there's hardly a passionate flicker left in a vagina.

One of the few instances in which society seems able to condone sensuality in a woman is when she is "taken" and overwhelmed by the male. It is under these circumstances, in which the man assumes total responsibility for the figurative rape, that a woman can shed her guilts about enjoying sex. Even in long-standing relationships, many women can achieve sexual satisfaction only when they fantasize they're being raped. Here, too, they mustn't lose control. It cannot be their desire; it has to be someone else's bestiality. Every woman understands, in Molly Haskell's words, that resistance has become "the woman's signal that she is virtuous and therefore worthy of conquest."[6] This is probably why so many women identified with Scarlett O'Hara when Rhett Butler, ignoring her screaming protests, swept her in his arms and carried her up the staircase.

Where did this mythology start?

Why has female sexuality been washed away? Why is the multi-orgasmic woman feared? Why has male prowess been eroticized and female passivity encouraged? What is the origin of the stereotypical pattern which dictates that a good woman/mother/homemaker must be nonsensual?

How could it be that only a few generations ago many people "found it impossible to believe that normal women might have orgasms"?[7]

You Used to Have It, Girls

There are legends about female sexuality dating back to the Neolithic period which suggest that it was women, and not men, who were considered to be more active sexually. These tales say that women were highly orgastic and indulged excessively in "orgastic parties."* The double standard operated then in reverse. Women were said to have relations with several different men during a single day.

Some historians suggest that it was due to concerns about property and inheritance laws that the institution of marriage was first introduced. In order to authenticate rights of inheritance, the issue of paternity became important, and female promiscuity could not be tolerated. It was said that if female sensuality were unleashed and allowed to flourish, marriage would collapse; paternity could not be validated; chaos and disintegration of the established order would result.

---

* It is interesting to compare this ancient data with the sexual responsivity of higher primates, whose sexual anatomy is so similar to that of the human female. Notes Dr. Mary Jane Sherfey in "The Evolution and Nature of Female Sexuality in Relation to Psychoanalytic Theory": "Having no cultural restrictions, these primate females will perform coitus from twenty to fifty times a day during the peak week of estrus, usually with several series of copulations in rapid succession. If necessary, they flirt, solicit, present, and stimulate the male in order to obtain successive coitions. They will 'consort' with one male for several days until he is exhausted, then take up with another. . . . I suggest that something akin to this behavior could be paralleled by the human female if her civilization allowed it."

Men Are Different??!!

However, it was believed that only female sensuality had to be contained and controlled. Men were thought to be wiser and more responsible, so they could handle anything. *But not women!* Men could be sexual without threatening the sanctity of the family structure. *But not women!* Men could be active, sensual beings and still lead sensible lives as dignified people. *But not women!*

In the nineteenth century, a famous physician, Sir William Acton, wrote a number of sexological books arguing his thesis on female sexuality. He maintained that "the majority of women (happily for them) are not very much troubled with sexual feeling of any kind. . . . The best mothers, wives, and managers of households, know little or nothing of sexual indulgence. Love of home, children, and domestic duties, are the only passions they feel. As a general rule, a modest woman seldom desires any sexual gratification for herself. She submits to her husband, but . . . would far rather be relieved from his attentions."

He went on to argue that to impute sexual feelings to a woman was a "vile aspersion." However, he did concede that women in the lower classes may have experienced such emotions.

Modern research data has long since exploded such myths, suggesting, in fact, that women who have gone to graduate or professional school are the most sexual women in our society.

Kenneth Davidson's study at the Medical College of Georgia and at Augusta State College have found that educated women report a higher incidence of orgasm on a regular basis, that they have a more favorable attitude toward participating in oral-genital sex and masturbation, and that they are more likely to have participated in sex during the menstrual period.

Dr. Harriet Lerner of the Menninger Clinic in Topeka, Kansas, adds that women who are intellectually active tend to have higher self-esteem, and that with higher self-esteem they tend to feel more sexual. In fact, confirmation from numerous sources validates that intelligent women are more sensual.

With the preponderance of data available, it is curious to note that so many worn, ridiculous beliefs about the female's lack of sensuality still shackle some so-called enlightened thinkers. As a result, many women still feel sexually *inferior* to men. They subscribe to the notion that sensuality, sex and having orgasms are exclusive and appropriate only to the emotional disposition and physical anatomy of men.

Few people understand the fundamental psychological and physiological similarities between men and women.* After years of working with normal patients and discussing their sexual anxieties, expectations and problems, I find that men and women report few, if any, psychological or emotional differences in experiencing their sexuality.

I've also found that there is a remarkable similarity in the frequency, desire, motivation, excitement, joy, and fear of sexuality in men and women. The way in which men patients speak of their needs in relation to caressing, kissing, sensitivity to touch, and orgasm are markedly similar to women as well. Many of my male

* During the first six weeks of fetal life the male/female genitalia are identical. And it is not until the seventh week of embryonic development that differentiation begins and the male genitalia start to take on their male characteristics. Even the functioning of many muscles and sphincters in the male/female genitalia are similar.

patients, for example, have acknowledged that they enjoy the same feelings of arousal as women do at having their breasts kissed and stroked. For women to believe that they have different sexual needs or requirements from men simply shows a misunderstanding of the nature of the biological properties of evolutionary and morphogenetic processes.

Freud Helped Women Feel Sexually Inferior, Too

Women's sexuality wasn't completely stamped out by societal prohibitions, and misinformation. Freud entered the picture in the late 1800s to contribute his share. His theories about "mature" female sexuality caused many women to feel guilty and inadequate. In his "vaginal transfer" theory, he postulated that a truly mature woman would achieve orgasm during vaginal penetration alone. To need anything else was a sign of incomplete psychosexual development. He even carried his argument to an extreme by claiming that nonvaginal sources of erotic pleasure were "polymorphously perverse" (or childlike) in origin and therefore infantile. He further inhibited female sexuality by suggesting that man, when sexually aroused, becomes aggressive, and that sexually aroused women should become submissive.

Through Freud's negative influence thousands of women decided that whatever their "favorite way" of reaching a climax was—it was wrong and immature.

It was Dr. Abraham Brill, the earliest translator of Freud's literary works in America, who scoffed at the master's theory of vaginal transfer. But Dr. Brill was too loyal to openly criticize the man whom he otherwise venerated.

Finally, in 1899, Denslow Lewis, a Chicago gynecologist, made observations similar to those of Brill and spoke of the role of the clitoris in orgasm. Then in 1952 Dr. Judd Marmor, former president of the American

Psychiatric Association, became the first psychoanalyst to openly question Freud's vaginal transfer theory. Dr. Sandor Rado, who founded the Psychoanalytic Clinic at Columbia University, also negated Freud's views on female sexuality. Rado followed Marmor's lead and pointed to the important role of the clitoris in achieving orgasm. They explained that the clitoris housed a dense concentration of nerve endings, whereas the vaginal walls were largely devoid of the nerve endings that transmit pleasurable sensations.

More recent support for the critical role of the clitoris in orgasm came from the findings of Masters and Johnson. They proved that the clitoris is the primary organ of female eroticism—the only organ whose sole purpose is to provide this pleasure.

Women were saved! They were able to come out of hiding, expressing their desire for clitoral stimulation without being labeled immature or perverse.

Your Entire Body—Sensual!!

In the PLEASURE PROCESS, female sexuality takes another step forward. Building on the research of Masters and Johnson, and others, my technique can help modern woman to return to her natural, biologically determined position of being a highly orgasmic and sensual person . . . with the dignity and self-esteem a woman deserves.

Not only the clitoris, but the entire body can become a source of erotic pleasure. Once a couple learns to go through the steps of the PLEASURE PROCESS, dozens and dozens of orgasms will be enjoyed. A woman will be able to do this just by being held and stroked. Rubbing the skin and caressing the body in areas that were formerly thought to be nonerotic (e.g., fingers, the back, the feet, etc.) will induce orgasm.

Early confirmation of the erotic possibilities that are available to you in the PLEASURE PROCESS were first observed by Dickinson and Beam. Their research records contain "instances of orgasm obtained from nipple suction, from lying beside another, from nursing a baby, from pressing (fully dressed) against another, from a shampoo at the hands of a male hairdresser, from a look, from a kiss, from touching the eye or the ear, from a handclasp, and from a picture of a flower which contains no figure and no likeness to any person or scene."[8] Does this sound unbelievable to you?

In the PLEASURE PROCESS you will learn how to orgasm in countless ways and in countless numbers. You will learn skills that will allow "the highest unfolding of [your] creative powers not through asceticism but through sexual happiness."[9]

The High Cost of Repression

You may be thinking to yourself, "I've gotten along all these years without being so sensual and without all this focusing on sex, and I've lived a very full and happy life. I'm satisfied." And I understand what you're saying. But there's a psychological maxim I want to share with you. There is no way to repress *only* your sensuality.

The mechanism of repression is so comprehensive in terms of personality constriction, it's analogous to a keyboard. On a keyboard there are dozens of octaves and 88 keys. Let us say, for example, that the symbol for sensuality is the middle key, "C." And you think, "Okay, I don't want to bother with sensuality. I am happy the way I am. I'm going to push down just 'C' and repress only that one key."

Well, psychologically there is no way to push down just the key of "C." On the contrary, you may as well take your arms from your elbows to your hands and lean forward, pressing down on the keyboard. As you put your arms onto the keyboard in an attempt to repress just "C," you will accidentally repress about three octaves of feelings. So when you're trying to repress sensuality, you're also inadvertently repressing other sensual experiences such as eating, touching soft forms and angular objects, watching the sunset, taking a shower and feeling the warm water on your body, the sensual experience of looking at beauty, the sensual experience of listening to music.

What I'm saying is that there is no way psychologically to repress just the note "C" on your keyboard. When you repress sensuality, you repress several other octaves of feelings and sensations, as well. So the cost of this repression is great. You think you're just pushing down one single emotional key. You're not. Your entire life is restricted because of your attempts at repression. Putting the brakes on your sensuality will do much more than you bargained for. The cost is just too great.

Give Yourself a Chance

All of us on this beautiful earth are terminal; no one is getting out of here alive. Your visa is stamped; your days are numbered. A healthy and rewarding sex life, however, can be critical to your overall picture of physiological and psychological adjustment.

There are many ingredients that blend into the potpourri of a stable personality and lead to maximum personality development, emotional growth and feelings of self-worth. They include:

—self-respect and self-pride,
—self-acceptance and self-love,
—commitment to a meaningful and exclusive love relationship,
—a family to love and identify with,
—work that is fulfilling, and
—a caring concern for and responsibility to the community.

One more ingredient is of primary importance to complete this ideal list: a healthy and active sex life.

Too many women I've treated repress their normal sexual functioning. Their pleasure in sex is rare or non-existent—a mundane fare tolerated at highly infrequent intervals.* Often a closer examination of their emotional profiles reveals that these sexually sterile women have rigid and peculiar personalities, as well.

Even women who *do* enjoy themselves sexually report that they experience long periods of distancing and loneliness following the closeness and intimacy of being sensually connected with their mates. These periods of distancing are caused (supposedly) by fights over children, money, friends, work, or nonsensical issues that cannot even be remembered later. Whatever causes are credited to the arguments and separations after sex, *too few people* are able to experience more than ephemeral flights into passion and sensuality without following them with extended episodes of fighting, silence or some other kind of withdrawal.

---

* Research indicates that as much as 50 percent of the female population has some kind of sexual dysfunction.

YOU CAN LEARN TO STOP THESE PAINFUL
DISTANCING PATTERNS

You can incorporate a healthy festival of sexuality into your lifestyle. Learn how to expand your territories and your ability to endure pleasure at more frequent intervals; stretch your capacity to tolerate more joy in sex. Give yourself a chance to take a look and see what is on the other side of the mountain. The sensuality you will discover there will compare to an "out-of-this-planet" excursion into a kaleidoscope of beauty, fantasy and wonderment. You'll find that after pleasure comes *more* pleasure. And after *more* pleasure you can learn to experience *much more* pleasure.

"Insteads" for Sex

When you repress your normal sexual needs, you unwittingly create substitutes, or "insteads," to replace them. These "insteads" surface into your life disguised as physical and emotional problems and include many of the physical complaints that women suffer from. Symptoms such as menstrual cramping, headaches, backaches, acne, asthma, dizziness, depression, vaginal rashes, and generalized feelings of anxiety and discomfort are common to the women I've treated who are anorgastic and/or frigid. However, in therapy, once they have learned to enjoy themselves more sexually, these problems tend to clear up. Even symptoms that seem completely unrelated, such as hyperactivity, overeating, overdrinking or overworking, may come under control because the total personality can be affected when a woman feels good about herself. When she can experience increased sexuality and femininity, she also accrues a sense of increased pride and self-confidence.

The Status Quo: Good Enough?

Typically when new patients come into therapy they say, "My sexual life is good. In fact, it is so satisfying that I'm not even interested in making changes. I don't need things to improve because I'm already having two or three orgasms—all anyone could ask for—and I'm quite happy."

If that is your story . . .

THAT'S FINE—but hang on and hang in.

How many among you have experienced the optimum in sexuality: *complete* emotional and physical satiation? And how many among you have ever heard of an orgasm called the *"'maxi'"*?* Few women in the world have. Most women understand very little about the amazing potential of the female sexual anatomy. Even those women who lead otherwise healthy and effective lives are filled with gnawing anxieties and doubts about their sexuality. They are so preoccupied with self-criticism and self-hate that there is little time left for pleasure. It is difficult for them to put their negative feelings to rest long enough to enjoy intercourse, and they are fraught with the ego-destructive tyrannies of performance anxieties and worries about frigidity. One of my patients explained:

> I am so rankled worrying about terrors like my
> dry vagina that I can't relax; my head is too mud-
> dled thinking: "What if he notices that I'm not

---

* The *maxi*-orgasm is described in detail in the chapter entitled "101 Orgasms."

lubricating yet? Does he find me as appealing as what's-her-name? Is he not getting hard because I've gained so much weight? If only I had douched! Would he cheat on me if I stopped feigning orgasms? Should I be moving faster/slower/more to the left? Do other women talk more or less—do they sigh, groan, pant, or are they quieter?"

Most of the women I talk to fear that every other woman they know is more informed, more skilled, more "sexy" and more desirable than they are.

On every continent where I've worked, doing television and radio shows and answering listeners' calls and letters, I've heard the same questions asked. Women have concerns about their sexuality. Long before James Joyce unleashed the four-letter word in *Ulysses,* the most common problems people everywhere have wanted to discuss have related to their sexuality.

If your mind is cluttered with doubts and questions when you're having sex, if you're fretting and agonizing about the "if only's," "what if's," "shoulds" and "woulds," you're probably too involved in an intellectual conversation with yourself to let any sexual feelings seep through.

It is time now for you to *be good to you*: it is time to stop the iron club of criticism that is pounding in your head; it is time for you to try something new.

Join Hands

I want you to take my hand and join hands with my other patients, too. Their progress will be yours; their insights and therapy will be yours, too. As they develop and change, so will you. Come along now and:

—*Listen to your precious erotic child:*
Uncover the vast storehouses of *buried sensuality* that are waiting in the beautiful hidden room of your unconscious; release and appreciate the erotic child hiding within you.

—*Explore your childhood fantasies:*
Unearth the fantasies, dreams, and private preferences and expectations that comprise your *individual hallmark* of sexuality.

—*Discard archaic notions:*
Rid yourself of the old *myths, inhibitions* and *taboos* that you incorporated into your thinking when you were a small child.

—*Eliminate the terrors:*
Put to rest the *unrelenting fears* of needing to perform and please. Put away your anxieties about frigidity and be as orgasmic as you like.

—*Change your focus:*
Learn how to *focus on yourself* and receive the sensory stirrings of your body; get into the *now* and the immediacy of your loving experiences.

—*Banish the negatives:*
Develop a positive world for yourself and become your own source of *approval* and *respect*. Others will follow your model and give you positives, too.

—*Be an original:*
Discover the power and beauty of your *authentic self;* dare to be the *real you.* You're the only one of a kind, a rare original.

—*Feel your entire body as sensual:*
Get in flight as you *listen to your skin.* Experience

your entire body becoming a tingling erogenous zone.

—*Discover that silence isn't golden:*

Get acquainted with other sensual options: talk and have fun during sex, using a special kind of nonsensual language from your past. It will reveal your *personalized signature* of erotica.

—*Share imagery:*

Get in touch with lost erotic memories from childhood—beautiful imagery that is locked up now in your subconscious. Let it all come out and play so you can *share* with your lover.

—*Appreciate the romance of the soft-on:*

Throw away the notion that good sex is dependent on your partner's being an *olympic athlete*—a superjock with an eternal erection. Discover the romance of the soft-on.

—*Explode the fiction:*

It is nonsense to assume that sexual desire and capacity *wither with age*. You can become more sensual and sexual every day of your life.

Give Yourself Something Special

F. Scott Fitzgerald reputedly once observed, "Almost all normal people want to be rich and famous without great effort." As adults, you and I know this isn't possible. Similarly, to accomplish the aims of this book, effort *does* need to be expended, and you're the only one who can make it happen *for you.*

DO IT—YOU'RE WORTH IT!

You deserve the pleasure.
You deserve to be a *happy, fulfilled* woman.

I want you to put forth the effort and see how much fun you will have. By learning simple techniques and exercises which include easy-to-understand procedures for HUGGING and FINGERTIPPING, your whole body— the entire surface of your skin—can become an erogenous zone. Not just the special areas we've been led to believe are erotic. Every nerve ending can become sensitized to the sensual experience: your shoulders, your cheeks, your fingers, your toes—everything! You'll be able to orgasm as easily with someone touching your back as you will when someone touches your clitoris. And afterwards you will revel in complete contentment and peace with yourself—feeling energetic and refueled, ready to tackle a busy schedule at work or at home.

Every woman can get in touch with these invigorating feelings of pride. Each of you can learn to express your individuality and sensuality as you learn how to love and trust yourself and put aside your fears. Imagine— an educational experience where you can learn about yourself, give yourself something special, and feel good at the same time!

Even though you will be having fun with the simple exercises and homework I've prepared for you, I call the activities we will undertake together "work." Because I love my work so much, the word *work* has happy, positive connotations for me. And the work we will be involved in, as I tell my patients, is talking and sharing. As my patients talk, work, and do their homework, so can you. You'll be probing into your sexual history, thinking about new ideas, and developing new physical, verbal and nonverbal skills. These changes will inspire and delight you as they start cropping up into your own behavior; they will encourage you to experiment more.

My methods are simple. The exercises are designed in an easy, step-by-step fashion. You can practice them whenever you like and move along at whatever pace is most comfortable for you.

Every woman reading this book can learn how to make her sexual hopes and fantasies become living realities. You can stop comparing yourself negatively with other women; you don't need to feel different or inadequate anymore. You can be the exciting, sensual woman you've envied in books and seen in films.

I'll be your guide. Come take my hand now and join me as we embark on this fascinating journey into you. Discover the extravaganza of sensuality that awaits you when you welcome the miracle of efficiency, coordination and engineering precision you inhabit—your healthy body. Learn to use and appreciate your fundamental biological equipment as the very remarkable and feminine you emerges. Function in an ideal sexual way.

BE A COMPLETE WOMAN . . .

a total woman who can embrace herself with greater confidence, personal integrity and feelings of increased self-worth.

YOU DESERVE ALL OF THIS . . . AND NOW!

PART ONE:

BURIED TREASURES

Chapter 1

You . . .
The Erotic Child

I seek for one as fair and gay,
But find none to remind me,
How blest the hours pass'd away
With the girl I left behind me.

—UNKNOWN

Your unique sexual personality is part of you from the moment of birth. Right from the very beginning you have sensual behaviors that are instinctive. They appear without any exposure to prior education or modeling. They are the gift of your genetic endowment, your natural birthright.

"Your erotic instinct," said Carl Gustav Jung, "belongs to the original nature of man. . . . It is connected with the highest form of spirit."

From your earliest beginnings your first erotic behavior—sucking—is established. It is necessary for the maintenance of life, critical to your survival. As soon as you are placed on your mother's breast you know what to do. Your behavior is instinctive. Society's judgmental values haven't yet contaminated your thinking. You have no fear or anxiety about your sensuality when you are newborn. You revel in it as you grab on to the nipple. It's delicious, the nectar of life. And it's all yours.

Even before birth, as an embryo inside your mother's body, you are enclosed in a "comforting cocoon of sensuality."

> Our first home, the womb is a highly sensual, intimate environment. Bathed in the warmth of the amniotic fluid, gently rocked by our mother's movements, comforted by the rhythm of the maternal breathing and heartbeat, we wait. . . .[10]

In the womb you wait until your birth. Then it is the nipple, sensual and life-giving, that becomes your first interpersonal connection to another human being; it also becomes your first erotic connection. Long before speech, before social skills, or before you begin the struggle of understanding your gender or your role as a female, you are a sensual being.

As a newborn child you enter into an almost totally sensual world. Daily you are oiled and bathed, hugged, rocked, petted and kissed. Even complete strangers pick you up, fondle and play with you. Your body becomes public domain. Affectionate caretakers are constantly stimulating and caressing you. As you learn to appreciate the language of these gentle caressing hands, you soon discover how to imitate them. With simple innocence and openness you explore. Your sensuality actually starts in your crib, where you quickly catch on and learn how to recreate the delightful experience for yourself—fondling and touching your own body.

This self-discovery and sensual pleasuring is normal, healthy and universal. Even a publication as conservative as The American National Red Cross Instructor's Guide includes material suggesting that "sexual awareness begins in infancy. Infants derive pleasant feelings from stroking [their] genitals." Experts on the developmental stages of childhood agree that masturbation is a natural function which is developmentally the prelude to normal, adult sexuality.

Cross-culturally medical researchers have observed babies as young as six months of age masturbating and having what appear to be full orgasmic responses. Kinsey gives this graphic description of a three-year-old girl masturbating to orgasm:

> There were 44 thrusts in unbroken rhythm, a slight momentary pause, 87 thrusts followed by a slight momentary pause, then 10 thrusts, and then a cessation of all movement. There was marked concentration and intense breathing with abrupt jerks as orgasm approached. She was completely oblivious to everything during these later stages of the activity. Her eyes were glassy and fixed in a vacant stare. There was noticeable relief and relaxation after orgasm.[11]

The developmental literature abounds with records of childhood sensuality. Children experience sexual excitement. That infants can experience intense erotic feelings is shown by the occurrence of masturbations culminating in orgasm.

The late Dr. Harry Bakwin cites the cases of five children referred to G. F. Still for masturbation who were under one year of age, and six who were in the second year of life. These children had been observed masturbating by placing toys and dolls against their bodies, by making rhythmic movements against pillows, or by crossing their legs and rocking. In Bakwin's own practice he encountered similar instances of infant masturbation.

Freud first advanced his revolutionary essays on childhood sexuality in 1905. He gave scientific respectability to the theory that even small children are deeply involved with sexual phenomena, at both the psychological and the physiological levels. While studies in the research on early childhood development suggest that this is normal, pediatricians still receive calls from troubled parents who frantically express concern because they have found their babies engrossed in fondling themselves and stimulating their genitals.*

It was your loving parents, anxious and guilt-ridden about their own sensuality, who unwittingly suppressed your instinctive erotic behaviors. Most parents remember too well their own childhoods and the scoldings they received from their parents. Because of their own anxieties and unfortunate early indoctrination about anything closely approximating sensuality, the entire subject had to be considered verboten, dirty and bad.

The fact is that masturbation is part of normal, healthy behavior, starting with infancy and usually continuing through adulthood. There is general agreement among psychologists that:

> Masturbation is not harmful physically or mentally unless it produces feelings of guilt from ingrained misconceptions. Masturbation is indeed a part of adolescent sexual development and should be regarded as such. If the parents feel it a deviance they will convey their feelings to the adolescent, however strenuously they attempt not to reveal them. This can lead to guilt and an inability for full sexual expression. Kinsey's data demonstrate that women who had experienced orgasm by any means prior to marriage achieved heterosexual responsiveness with greater ease than those who had not.[12]

As a child you have to accept your parents' myths and prejudices and adapt to their standards of "appro-

---

* Perhaps it would be good for parents to note that McCary's studies have shown that children with a history of regular masturbation demonstrate heightened heterosexual behaviors.

priate" behavior. You memorize word for word the negative labels your parents attach to sensuality, whether it is expressed in feelings, ideas, activities, dreams—whatever. It is all classified FORBIDDEN: masturbation, sexual discovery and play, fantasies, intimacy, touching, orgasm—

ALL ARE FORBIDDEN.

Parents teach, pressure and punish their impressionable children until most signs of sexual life are dead. Sensuality is destroyed by their horrified looks and comments: "Where did you put your fingers last? Yecch! Go wash your hands at once." Everyone else has license to feel you—everyone else can touch you—everyone except you.

Do Not Disturb

As a child you are too young to fathom what sexuality means in adult terms or why there are so many negative reactions from them and so much fear. You have neither the background nor the understanding to make sense out of what is happening. Swamped with misinformation and misconceptions, you are forced to deal with a maze of unknowns and confusions. Staffed with naivete and ignorance about sexuality, you are caught up into a seemingly irresolvable dilemma. Your body tells you that all the pleasant sensations you feel when you caress yourself and play with your genitals are *good*. But at the same time you are processing the parental message that comes out loud and clear: "What you are doing is *bad*." Since no conflict with authority figures can be tolerated, you must cease and desist. Sensuality is punishable by law—*parental law*.

TOUCHING YOURSELF IS PROHIBITED.

You listen, you obey. Too soon your erotic child dies—your sensuality erodes away. It dissolves a little each day until all evidence is wiped out. Then a sign goes up on your genitals which reads:

PLEASE DO NOT DISTURB.

Parental influences have lifelong damaging effects on your adult sexual behaviors. Experts on sexual development believe that our negative early parent/child interactions concerning sex are so important that they shape the direction of our future lives.

SARAH AND HER BABY BLANKET

Sarah and Leon had been married seven years when they came in to see me to discuss their sexual problems. Sarah was worried because, although she loved her husband Leon, they had sex only three or four times a year. And then it happened only when she had too much to drink or they were away on holiday. It was at these special times when her defenses were low and her guard was down that they would have sex.

At home, their most intimate moments were shared over the phone, when Leon called Sarah from his office. They had great fun during these conversations, and they could both speak affectionately. Sarah would enjoy so many romantic feelings about Leon that she would go into the bedroom after these conversations and masturbate. Her style of masturbating was always the same. It was a ritual she had been doing since she was a child. She would manipulate her baby blanket (which she always kept hidden in a corner of her closet) by pull-it back and forth between her legs until she had an orgasm.

In the course of her therapy Sarah recalled a painful incident which happened when she was about three years old. She had been curled up in a comfortable chair, watching her favorite television program. She was so engrossed in the program that she didn't realize she was fondling her genitals. The child was startled when her mother burst into the room shouting, "What are you doing?"

Her mother's sudden anger was a shock. Sarah was frightened when her little hands were slapped.

"Stop it at once! Don't ever touch yourself down there!"

The mother's hysterical intrusion made such an impression on Sarah that she never again touched her genitals unless she was eliminating or bathing. To satisfy her normal sexual needs she found another way. She figured out how to use her blanket to pleasure herself.

Sarah never forgot her mother's words; they had made a lasting imprint on her memory. Even as a married woman, neither she *nor* her husband could touch her "down there" unless she was drunk or on a vacation. Sarah had learned her early lesson too well; she had memorized the FORBIDDENS and was unable to reverse the process until years later when she came into my office to work on her problems in therapy.

Why are we so influenced by our parents? Why do we accept without question all their views and distortions about our sexuality? Because we have no other options. Our parents are the only show in town. They are our major source of approval and nourishment. Because we're totally dependent on them for our life support systems, we throw in the towel and do it their way. We consciously, as well as unconsciously, absorb everything they say. We digest all their values and judgments about sex and incorporate them into our own value systems. We conform to their models of acceptable behavior and we mimic their rituals and repeat their rules: no more overt sensuality, no more spontaneity, no more fun.

Banishing the Erotic Child

Your parents' words make their mark, like water . . . dripping . . . wearing away at stone. You, the erotic child, are banished—you go underground. You and your guilt retreat into a subterranean world of your unconscious. The "DO NOT DISTURB" signs your parents have engraved on your mind block out your early memories, leaving behind only feared remnants of disapproval and punishment.

When you're small, you hear too much of "Take your hands away from there! Don't touch yourself! That's dirty!"

These kinds of phrases become forever associated with your genitals, because whenever your hands did find their way down to that little place between your legs, one of your parents was usually there to pounce on you and grab your hands away. After several pounces and reprimands, you got the idea! There was indeed something awfully dirty and smelly down there, and you knew you had better keep your hands away from it.

From then on, whenever you found yourself playing with your little vagina (because it felt so good), you suddenly moved into an alert stage and reminded yourself of what your parents said—that that kind of activity was really wrong. More than wrong, touching yourself down there was about *the worst thing you could do.*

When you finally became an adult and the scolding parent (or the reminding parent) was no longer there, whenever your hand found your genitalia, a screaming alert in your subconscious rushed into action. It is much like a fire-alarm siren, even though no one hears it but you. It screeches out its message: DON'T TOUCH!

In your teens, your training becomes even more severe. Not only shouldn't *you* touch anything down there, but if you let any of those boys so much as *talk* about it, that will make you a fallen woman, a slut, and you will lose forever your "nice girl" status. After years and years of this sort of training, it's very hard to reverse your thinking.

Yet, the minute you get married, the message is reversed and you're told, "Go to it, kid. Everything is fine now, legal and proper. Be a voluptuous, sexy siren and please your man. Do it right—and do it right *now*!"

Just how do you make that sort of instant reversal? How do you wipe out all those years of judgmental, rigorous and absolute training?

Well, some women never do. They're the women who either never orgasm or accidentally manage to slip into one when the moon is facing Venus or in equinox.

But fortunately there is magic and wonder in the perfect engineering and construction of your mind. There is a "fail-safe" mechanism built into your subconscious which prevents your erotic history from being entirely erased. So that in reality, none of your sensual history is truly lost. Your natural erotica and femininity are *not* destroyed.* They stay imprinted on your mem-

---

* I have used the word *erotica* in this text to represent the compilation of all the erotic behaviors, memories, interactions and symbols from childhood which comprise an individual's sensual history.

ory. What happens is that you gather your FORBIDDENS together and store them away in your unconscious like toys in an attic. Like the princess in the fairy tale who waits for that special kiss, your erotica simply goes to sleep.

But even as your early infantile erotica sleeps, you still need to find a place to house the new, ongoing sensual feelings that continue to occur daily. Because the affectionate physical input from loving caretakers does not stop, the erotic feelings that result from these interactions do not stop (in spite of all the parental threats and punishments).

While intimacy, warmth and affectionate caressing from the outside world are necessary for the health, growth and development of a normal child, they will be destructive unless the child is given an emotional license from his parents to experience and enjoy the sensuality that results. Appropriate outlets need to be allowed by parents to release these feelings.

When children have the freedom to openly discuss their reactions with their parents, to work through their fantasies in play, to masturbate in privacy and be able to touch and enjoy their own bodies, then sensual stimulation from the environment becomes a healthy part of their total experience. But in most families discussing sexual feelings and masturbating (or engaging in any kind of self-stimulation) are strictly FORBIDDEN. So the child has to cope with solving a seemingly impossible dilemma.

Weaving Your Tapestry of Veiled Sensuality

In order to deal with the physical and emotional contradictions of the "yes-yes's" from your body feelings and the "no-no's" from your parents, unconsciously you, the erotic child, figure out what seems to be a practical solution. Covertly, you get the contact you need by sliding down banisters; climbing poles and jungle gyms; straddling furniture, toys or people; riding piggyback, horses, bikes, dogs or anything else you can; sitting with your thighs tightly crossed or holding yourself tightly between your legs; or reporting vaginal rashes and injuries to mother that require numerous gentle applications of emollients and powders.

You, the erotic child, also take care of another area —the emotional stimulation you need—by unconsciously associating and attaching some of your sensual feelings to innocuous, nonsensual objects in the environment which can serve as acceptable substitutes: pipes, trees, pistols, towers, tubes, tall buildings, furry objects, soft fabrics—the list is endless.

Most children learn as toddlers that they will feel safer when only *nonthreatening* symbolic representations of their sensuality emerge into awareness. It is too uncomfortable for them to deal with more obvious sensual realities that might elicit parental punishment and severe negative reactions later.

It is interesting to analyze the variety of symbolic substitutes that are used by patients who are working on sexual problems. These disguised images and objects frequently surface into view in dreams. In my cross-cultural work with patients I have found that the sexual symbolism in dreams is much the same: people see themselves running up *stairways;* climbing *tall trees;* shooting *long-barreled guns;* trying to escape through *winding hallways;* entering *large caverns,* et cetera. When we are awake, we sense that when erotic feelings do erupt, they are to be quickly disguised with benign symbols.

Occasionally, however, the disguises fail to function and the symbols take on real form. A patient described this experience to me.

NANCY'S "DANCING LOLLIPOPS"

For years a certain fantasy has popped into my head when my husband and I are having sex. I see lollipops dancing along in a chorus. Last night, when he was kissing my breasts, I saw them again. When I looked more closely I could see that the head of one of the lollipops was really the head of a penis. Then it changed and I saw that the testes were inverted and the stick of the lollipop was the penis. There were rows and rows of beautiful dancing penises with all the testes standing up. That scene in my head made me feel sexy—dancing "lollipops."

The emotional cover-ups and substitutions that can be invented are endless. As children, each of us learns how to weave our own tapestry of veiled sensuality. Instead of stroking genitals, we stroke pets; instead of playing doctor, we play with toys; instead of caressing our bodies, we caress dolls.

The covert psychological chicanery is the same. While our substitutes may take on different shapes and facades, their emotional purpose does *not* change: we hide from the world (and even from ourselves) the frequency and intensity of our sensual and sexual behavior. As we get older, the use of substitutes carries over into our adult lives. Representations of our sensuality can be seen in the symbolic long, sleek cars, the grand estates, the obsessive collections and the extravagant adult toys. Excessive allegiance to cults and social groups or fanatic religious involvements can also be used as substitutes for expressing our sensuality.

From Repression to Dysfunction

In childhood we learn to cut off our natural reservoir of sensual feelings. And, as the tragedy develops, the essentially denied child spawns the sexually inadequate adult. Denial acts as an unrelenting catalyst encouraging the growth of personality problems and feelings of inferiority. These problems gather strength during childhood and the stage is set for sexual dysfunction to take over.

A bizarre and unusual case I treated involving a young woman illustrates how serious sexual disorder can develop.

KELLY'S SELF-PUNISHMENT

Kelly was raised by older, severely punitive parents. She received no affection and a great deal of punishment for any breach of rules or etiquette. Once, when she was four years old, her father had found her masturbating in her bed. She was promptly beaten and locked in a closet overnight.

On another occasion, when she was eight, Kelly's mother discovered her rubbing herself between her legs as she lay reading. The punishment was sleeping outside on the doorstep for a week. "If you're going to act like a dog," her mother had said, "I'm going to treat you like a dog. And dogs sleep on the doorstep."

When Kelly came to see me she was twenty-eight

years old, had never married, and had had very little sex. The presenting problem was her concern about the way in which she masturbated. Kelly would insert wooden popsicle sticks into her vagina, then move them quickly in and out until she reached orgasm. This was her major source of sexual gratification, and she was worried that this sort of behavior was an indication of mental illness.*

In the course of our therapy Kelly realized that this behavior had begun soon after her father had beaten her for her "first offense." I explained to her that masturbating by using sticks that might injure her *was* bizarre and that it was due to the tremendous deprivation and punishment she had endured as a child.

When parents are severe in their repression of sensuality, their children grow into adults who feel so guilty about the sensual feelings they continue to have, that in order to experience their sensuality at all, they have to do it in a bizarre and/or painful manner. In fact, it is the parent who first teaches the child that the whole idea of sensuality is crazy or bizarre. The child then makes the connection that "if feeling sensual *is* crazy, I had better do it in a *crazy* way!"

And, as I explained to Kelly, the more guilt, repression, ignorance and denial that parents impose on their children, the more unusual will be the sexual practices these children engage in.

John Money, the authority on childhood sexuality and gender change, explains the critical impact that negative parent/child interactions concerning sex have

---

* C. E. Llewellyn describes a similar case where a guilt-ridden patient derived pleasure from masturbating by inserting rough sticks into her vagina and manipulating vigorously to orgasm. An examination by her gynecologist revealed marked lacerations and fissures, and secondary infection.

on later adult life. According to Dr. Money, when erotic growth and development have been distorted by too much inhibition, punishment and taboo, disorders arise including transvestism, or cross-dressing; transsexualism, a conflict over one's inner sexual identity; some kinds of homosexuality; and what science calls the paraphilias, popularly known as "kinky" sex. Best known of these are sadism and masochism, rape, exhibitionism, kleptomania, voyeurism, and fetishism. Still another class of sexual disorder is hypophilia, or sexual inadequacy.[13]

The more negatives and punishments that parents deliver, the more bizarre and unsatisfying are the sexual patterns that develop. In some cases, rigorous quantities of FORBIDDENS during childhood result in preventing the sex organs from functioning normally forever.

A case which poignantly illustrates how even in the first few months of life parental punishments can inhibit our feelings of sensuality is shown in this next case history.

AMY AND HER BATHINETTE

Amy had been a patient in my Tuesday night group for a year when she announced to the group that she was getting married. It was four months later that she and her new husband, Paul, came in for a private consultation. Paul was concerned that Amy couldn't have an orgasm when they made love. He knew she had experienced orgasms, but only by masturbating when she was alone.

Amy and Paul had been going together for three years before they married. It had been the same during their courtship: they had both enjoyed their sex, but Amy couldn't orgasm. However, they were happy together and Amy talked about Paul whenever she had an audience. She adored him and boasted to me:

> *He's the best lover I've ever had. Yet I still can't have an orgasm. I've never had one during sex with any man. How come? There's something so wrong with me! Even though I really love Paul, I don't want to have sex anymore. It makes me feel so inadequate, I just want to quit.*

One night in group, when Paul wasn't there, Amy explained that her pattern was a consistent one: she felt comfortable during their foreplay. She felt good when they were romantic, cuddling and kissing. She had always looked forward to being petted and fondled. But as the excitement increased and they began having intercourse, she would move into a panic and had to stop.

> *It's always the same. When we leave the leisurely kissing and hugging and the pace begins to accelerate, I start breathing faster and my hips begin to roll around. Then, like a motor switching off, I suddenly become still. I just lie there . . . rigid. A chill sweeps over me. Paul's hands suddenly seem different—strange—and it disgusts me to have them pressing against my body.*

> *It's so ominous. I can't stop the weird feelings that appear from nowhere. Paul's hands become evil. Then I think I'm going to suffocate. I ask him to orgasm and get it over with. I feel angry with myself and with him . . . cheated. I just don't want to have any more sex. It's too disappointing to get all excited, and then—nothing.*

Amy acknowledged that she hadn't shared these feelings with Paul. The group encouraged her to tell him. She finally agreed and explained it all to him in their private session with me.

I told them that I believed that something was bleeding through from Amy's childhood, something that frightened her whenever she approached orgasm. If she could uncover whatever it was that had happened to her as a child, it would *not* frighten her anymore. I believed that the material she was repressing was something quite innocent and pleasurable.

"It probably happened to you before you were two," I said. "And what terrible, ominous event could befall a lovely child at that young age? If you could stay with the feelings when the chill sweeps over you," I advised, "and share what's happening to you with Paul—and continue your lovemaking—I'm convinced that a part of your precious erotic child will reappear. But it will look healthy and normal to you now, because you're an adult."

I instructed Paul to be very tender and caressing when Amy became rigid and unresponsive during their lovemaking; to warmly encourage her to share her feelings; and to gently and slowly continue their sex. I urged him to hold off with his orgasm and not follow her instructions to "get it over with."

The next week they came in for their appointment holding hands and full of smiles. Amy was buoyant.

I did it! I had two!! Actual vaginal orgasms during intercourse!! *Can you believe it? We did just what you said, and when the chills and the fear came, I talked about everything that was happening to me. Paul just kept on loving me. He didn't miss a beat.*

*First I saw dozens of horrible hands. I thought
something evil would happen, but I kept talking.
Then it became foggy. Watching the image in my
head was like watching a film. The ominous hands
finally disappeared. Then I realized I was a baby
on my Bathinette, feeling so clean, chubby and
little. All at once everything seemed so pretty—I
felt so pretty.*

Amy said she was less than a year old in her image.
She saw her mother leaning over her. She had just finished having a bath. Lying on top of the Bathinette she
felt the soft towel as her mother patted her.

*She poured oil in the palm of her hands and gently
rubbed the oil all over my little fat body. The more
I talked about it as Paul made love to me—the
hotter I became. Those two orgasms just exploded
inside of me. It was like a wonderful miracle!*

Amy relived every minute of that warm, exquisite
daily ritual with her mother while she and Paul were
having intercourse. Then she made the connection:
when her husband caressed her, Amy unconsciously
flashed back to the sensual feelings of the Bathinette
and her mother's hands. Apparently her parent's negative facial expressions and judgmental words when she
touched herself had conditioned Amy's thinking even
before her first birthday. Even at that young age Amy
had understood that sensual feelings were "wrong" and
had to be banished.

Amy decided as a baby that the enjoyment of her
mother's hands on her body had to stop. She labeled her
sensual feelings "ominous/disgusting" and repressed
them deep into her unconscious. When she was having

intercourse, these old sensual feelings threatened to resurface. To defend against this threat and ensure that they remain repressed, a cold chill swept over her body signaling that danger was ahead. By terminating intercourse quickly and avoiding an orgasm, Amy was able to stop the guilt and shame that could have emerged if she remembered the Bathinette incident and how erotic she was as a small child.

Paul was happy to have been able to help Amy uncover some of the material that had kept her from being able to orgasm:

I always believed that our sex problems were all my fault. I've thought for over three years that Amy didn't orgasm because I was a lousy lover. I was afraid she would leave me eventually. I felt like such a failure at our sex.

Realizing that it was all those memories about the Bathinette that made her frightened has given me such a sense of relief. I feel better about myself and love her even more, understanding what she was all about as a child. And just thinking about it excites me!

Like Amy, in the chapters to follow you will learn how to discover your erotic child. Getting in touch with your lost sensual past will help to release the brakes on your sexuality. It will free you from the FORBIDDEN tapes and feelings of guilt and inadequacy that lead to the more commonly experienced problems and dysfunctions: inability to achieve orgasm, reduced sexual motivation and frigidity.

You can give yourself a full and satisfying sex life and you can do it *now*!

YOUR EROTIC NATURE IS YOUR BIRTHRIGHT.

Chapter 2

Your Beautiful
Hidden Room

I remember, I remember,
The house where I was born,
The little window where the sun
Came peeping in at morn . . .

—THOMAS HOOD

Within you there lies buried a wealth of erotica. It was hidden from your parents deep in your memory bank long ago. You stored it away for protection and safe-keeping. It has been lying in concealment all these years, like a lost treasure stowed in the hull of a sunken ship, waiting to be rediscovered.

The entire burial process was so unconscious that you may not even remember that this erotica exists—but it is with you today, longing to come out and play. It rests in a secret burial place in your psyche, in a grave that is unknelled and uncoffined. I call it the *beautiful hidden room* of your unconscious.

I know that the material that is locked up in the unconscious is beautiful. Over the years I've helped patients unearth the sensual bits and pieces in their hidden rooms, and in every case each piece has been precious—each piece has been *beautiful*. Because the majority of experiences that shape our sexual person-alities are hidden away from the first year of life to

60

about the fourth, it is easy to understand that they can consist only of the innocent, harmless interactions of a small child.

The following are examples of the sort of buried memories that some of my patients have shared:

I was about three and I was playing hide-and-go-seek. I was hiding in the shower when a man came in who was visiting my parents. He closed the bathroom door without realizing I was there. He urinated and I saw his penis. I was fascinated—but worried that he would catch me hiding behind the shower curtain, watching him.

I saw my mother's friend open her blouse and take her breast out. I was so surprised. The nipple was big and red and had little bumps around it. Then she put her baby's mouth next to it and I could see how he grabbed and sucked it. I wanted to feel it and suck it, too.

My mother was trying on bathrobes in the dressing room of a department store. As we walked down the corridor I tried to peek behind the curtains of each room so I could get a glimpse of a nude body.

Vignettes such as these don't sound earth-shattering. You wouldn't be jailed for sharing this kind of information. Yet people hide such experiences in their subconscious like guilty thieves secretly stashing away the evidence. Over the years these innocent bits grow in importance, corroding with layers and layers of guilt, until they take up so much space in our psyches there is no room left for pleasure.

Everyone has a different collection of unique pieces that lie hidden away. They form the mosaic of our individual sexual personalities. With the help of an experienced guide you can reenter *your* beautiful secret hiding place and unearth your riches. They are your rightful heritage, a dowry awaiting the marriage of your adult sensuality with your childhood eroticism. Once you can uncover your vast cache of sexuality, you'll find unlimited highs and surges of self-confidence waiting there for you, and feelings of intense joy and fulfillment.

Few of us know *how* to return and break through into our stronghold, so it is unlikely that our lost memories will ever surface into conscious awareness again. Too many of us live our lives never able to recover these treasures. Usually they lie in embarrassed retreat, gathering feelings of guilt and inadequacy until death do us part.

Many of my patients have shared that they have felt guilty just *thinking,* let alone *doing,* anything even slightly sexual. Here's how one patient explained her feelings to me.

LEAH'S "CRAZY" THOUGHTS

I just knew I was the only girl who was having crazy thoughts and ideas and sexy feelings. I felt uncomfortable being so different. None of the other girls at school were sharing erotic secrets or talking about their fantasies and daydreams. So I believed I was the only one who had them.

I felt peculiar. Ever since I can remember I've been sneaking around, hiding the guilt about everything I fantasized—things that I just knew were "dirty" and "wicked." But I never stopped fantasizing. I just got better at sneaking and hiding and feeling lousy about myself.

As new patients come into group therapy sessions and share their childhood secrets, they are surprised to find that everyone else in the group has experienced similar feelings. But we don't know this when we are children. Rather we are certain that we are different and peculiar. It is a surprise to hear other adults relating similar stories from their childhoods; it is a surprise to find out that we homo sapiens are so much alike.

When you can openly share and discuss your childhood sexual experiences and training with other adults, the pieces fall into place. The guilts and unknowns vanish and you can better understand how . . .

Today's Sexual Patterns Were Established Yesterday

When we're adults we assure ourselves that whatever our parents preached to us about sex when we were children had had very little influence upon us today. We're confident that our sexual behavior is *self-determined* now, an original pattern that we personally designed for ourselves. We think we are responsible for our own choices now. This just isn't true.

Most people have fixed behavioral systems which determine how they act during sex, and these were established from the network of bits and pieces they've hidden away. One person needs to be in the missionary position to orgasm. For another, it must be on the side or from the back. Should the lights be on or off? Do you do it in the morning or only at night? Do you want it in bed, on a boat, in the car, or on the floor? Each of us has a particular mode that feels right.

Whichever mode works best for you, it *wasn't* determined during your adulthood or even by *you*. All the sexual nuances—the setting and the accoutrements that make us feel comfortable, our practices, postures and preferences—are strongly linked to specific unconscious erotic interactions with our parents and to those hidden pieces that we have buried away since our early beginnings.

The amount of guilt, self-hate and self-deprecation we've stored in our subconscious affects the degree of sensuality we can tolerate as adults.

You weren't allowed to cast your vote when your sexual personality was first molded. It was all decided for you and fixed by the time you were four years old. Your present practices, prejudices and values about sex derived from the unfortunate models you listened to, the distorted myths and old wives' tales you absorbed and the guilts you incorporated.

Even as adults it is difficult for us to behave sensually, because the little child inside each of us still fears that the censoring parent will suddenly emerge to criticize and punish. Long after parental influence is gone, we still tend to act like frightened children, stuffing our FORBIDDEN secrets away and behaving like the non-sensual, sterile beings we were raised to be.

But you can break the mold; you can *stop* paralyzing your sexual joy; you can *stop* pleasing mommy and daddy with your frigidity and sexual sterility. They don't care about your sex life anymore.

It's time for you to reawaken and get moving; it's time to realize you're sitting there all alone holding on to those dead genitals; it's time to go back and . . .

Take a Second Look

Start to change. You can, now, by taking a second look. You can unlock the doors of your beautiful hidden room and redesign your life. Drawing upon your adult frame of reference, you need to revisit your unconscious and look around again. This is the key: going back and recovering your lost childhood sensuality. And, you must go back as an *accepting* adult, not the *frightened* child.

BE POSITIVE AND TRUST YOURSELF.

Change occurs in a warm bath of you trusting *you*, and you being *positive* to you. Being negative or critical of yourself will destroy your motivation, keep you down and depressed, and prohibit change. So be very *positive* to yourself as you learn to respect yourself and understand that whatever you feel or have felt as a child sexually is good, wonderful, normal, and healthy.

A new assessment needs to be made of your childhood history and experiences. But this reevaluation needs to be made by someone who can be positive, just and fair. You'll need to invite a stable, kind mediator —a wise judge. You already know a wonderful, special person to ask to join you: *invite you*!

Take a fresh look at your childhood sexuality with your *adult*, twentieth-century attitude and ability to reason. Reexamine the concepts and ideas you accepted when you were too young to evaluate their validity for yourself. Use your contemporary head and your mature eyes. Then you'll be ready to look at . . .

A Child's Innocent Capers

Your FORBIDDEN past is a series of innocent, childish capers. Go back and discover that the terrible secrets you've nurtured for so long are romantic and harmless. Then you'll realize that your erotic childhood escapades were whimsical, charming and completely normal. They will look innocent and playful when viewed with grown-up eyes. You'll be able to accept and enjoy how experimental and curious you were. The stigma and negative labels you and your parents levied long ago will vanish as you throw away the guards, fences and defenses you've erected. Use your early experiences and completely involve yourself in sexual feelings. You knew how when you were very small. You will again. It is *never* too late. Prepare now to take . . .

Your Magical Journey into the Past

It's time to start on your magical journey into the past and learn how to use the powerful erotic images from your beautiful hidden room. They can be called upon, invited to come out and play—to roam free. Transplant them so they can now embellish your adult sexuality.

We often get glimpses of these buried memories. They flash through our minds quickly like a motion picture flashing on and off the screen. At first they might appear blurry and almost unidentifiable, but gradually we can make out a vague scene, a figure, or a familiar place. It could be the face of a close relative, a friend, or an object. We're troubled by the way these images can just pop into our heads when we are warmly caressing and kissing our mates during sex. We assure ourselves they are meaningless and unimportant.

Right in the middle of lovemaking, these seemingly nonrelated, nonsensual images or fantasies can interrupt and flood your mind. You will probably be annoyed and find these images strangely obtrusive. People tend to ignore or push them away. When this happened to one of my patients during sex, she said she felt annoyed with herself and thought, "Why am I thinking of a flower? What's wrong with me? This isn't sexy!"

It is *no accident* that a particular image, object or thought may spring into your mind during sex.
It is *no accident* that these nonsexual images arrive precisely during the time your body is being stroked and your genitals are being stimulated.
This is *no coincidence*.

It is part of an early experience that is bleeding through from your past, daring to creep back into your thinking while you're having sex. The image was probably buried during a similar erotic moment when you were feeling sensual as a small child.

Making the Connection

By a process of pairing, or association, nonsexual objects and fantasies get linked up with our sensual feelings. They reappear into our awareness without warning. This can happen whenever the cues that originally introduced them are repeated.

For example, a child may be looking out of the window while massaging his genitals. The pleasurable body sensations become associated with the scene he is viewing. That is, the flowers outside, the sky and the trees may become paired with the ongoing experience of masturbation. Then the connection is made:

FLOWERS/TREES/SKY = GOOD FEELINGS,
STROKING OF
GENITALS,
ORGASM.

An entire grouping of nonsensual events gets connected up with sensual feelings. The flowers, trees and sky become the symbolic substitutes for the forbidden sexual experiences. They surface into consciousness, cautiously, during sensual play and physical stimulation. They slip into reality before the guard we've placed at the door of our unconscious realizes they've escaped. When this happens during sex we try to block them out so we can get back to enjoying ourselves.

STOP PUSHING THEM BACK. These so-called senseless, unrelated thoughts and images are a crucial link to your hidden erotica. Welcome them. Respect, cherish and value their reentry.

Give them a voice. Let these stunning images from your unconscious travel freely into the present. They represent the reservoir of sexual longings and unending passionate feelings for your unconscious. They are a breakthrough to the subtle remnants of the sexual material you repressed during childhood. While they may appear in a disguised form at first, if you can accept and talk about them now, they will play out their forgotten story.

Here are two case histories which illustrate how seemingly nonsensual images, when expressed during intercourse, can result in releasing a profusion of orgasmic responses.

CHARLOTTE AND THE PRAM

We were really getting into it, my husband and I. He was kissing and massaging me when all of a sudden I began seeing a stained-glass window.

I thought to myself, "Well, this sure isn't sexy, and even though Dr. Kassorla tells me to talk about everything that comes into my head when we have sex, this has got to be the wrong time to start talking about a window! Surely it will turn my husband off."

I tried to push the thought away, but the image kept flashing back into my head. My husband was caressing me, and I felt so good. Yet, I don't know why, this damned stained-glass window kept persisting!

Then I started remembering your words, Dr. Kassorla. I could hear you saying, "Get those pictures out; trust yourself; believe that the images in your head are good and that they won't hurt you, they'll help you. Get in touch with your buried feelings and talk about the symbolic images you see."

There I was, feeling and responding to my husband, hearing your words, and seeing a stained-glass window, all at the same time. Finally I thought, "What the heck, I'm going to give it a whirl."

"Honey," I said, "I see a beautiful stained-glass window; it is sort of dancing around in front of me."

As he was hugging me and kissing me I realized that just saying the words "stained-glass window" had made me hotter. I started coming! And my husband was only kissing my cheek. I couldn't believe it.

It was the first time in my life that I had ever had an orgasm when there were no hands or genitals or anything near my vagina. My husband was just kissing me, and there I was having an orgasm just

*by saying the words "stained-glass window." I
thought, "Well, hell, whatever this is, it's good!"
I felt encouraged, and I kept talking about what I
was seeing.*

*I suddenly realized I was in a room. It wasn't
dark, but it looked like sundown. I could hear
voices in another room. I realized I was very, very
little. I said out loud, "I'm so little and sweet. My
legs are so fat. I can feel how they are bent and
opened up." I realized I was a baby.*

*When I said to my husband, "Honey, I'm a baby,"
I felt myself coming again. Then he was sucking
my vagina and I was coming some more—so hard
and so deep I almost got frightened. But I tried to
just keep talking about what I was seeing.*

*Now my husband was inside me; he was stroking
me and I was having orgasms—in my life I've
never had so many. I couldn't count them. I didn't
care about counting. I just wanted to talk about
what I was seeing.*

*I said, "Hey, I'm in my pram. And I'm just so
cozy. Oh, my daddy is in the room, too. I can see
him, I can feel him. He's so tall. I can see his
silhouette against the window and he's looking at
me and smiling. He's kissing me now and petting
my face and saying, 'Oh, what a precious little
girl you are. You go have your nice little nap now,
honey.' "*

I explained to Charlotte that there must have been a
stained-glass window in the room where she was lying
in her pram. When her father came in, probably to
check and see if she was all right, she must have been

touching her vagina. Children often play with their genitals just before falling off to sleep. When her father walked in and kissed her, an association was made—a sensual connection was stamped into her subconscious tying her father's kissing her cheek to her enjoyment of playing with herself. Consequently, when her husband began touching her cheek, it immediately threw her back to the early memory of the stained-glass window. And, because she didn't try to repress it and wasn't afraid to talk about it, the old scene replayed.

When Charlotte was able to go back and grab that scene and make it come alive again in her contemporary sexuality, it allowed the orgasms to pour out of her, and in fact allowed the first orgasm to happen just by her being hugged. Now it's possible for her to have an orgasm with absolutely no attention to her genitals. But she had to make a verbal invitation to that old memory and give it permission to live in the present.

Case histories such as Charlotte described are common in my practice. Whenever those early memories are allowed to be aired in the present, intense feelings of sensuality follow.

HARRIET AND HER STORYBOOK FIGURES

For Harriet, a single woman I treated, the image which allowed her to make the connection between her erotic child and her adult sexuality centered on storybook figures:

> Before therapy, when things came into my head that were not seductive, I was afraid to talk about them. I was afraid the guy I was having sex with would think I was crazy. But one night I can remember getting more and more turned on as cer-

tain pictures started popping into my head. I don't know if it was my therapy, or the glass of wine I had earlier, or what—but I started seeing beautiful forms of people dressed in regal robes, and I started talking about them.

The forms looked like they were two-dimensional and made of wood. They were just wonderful to see as they drifted along, the way floats do in a parade. Each form resembled a character I had read about in a fairy tale when I was in grammar school. One was a beautiful princess with long, blonde hair. As I saw her go by I thought, "That's me!"

As we continued making love, whether he was kissing my breasts or my genitals or was inside of me, whatever was happening, I kept flashing back to these forms and talking about them, and he seemed to love it. As I continued, everything I said got me more excited and got him more excited, too, so I was encouraged to keep talking about whatever I was feeling and seeing.

One of the forms was a king, looking just like the one I saw in my favorite storybook when I was a little girl. He wore a crown and a beautiful fur-and-red-velvet robe. After he passed by, the queen came along and she was so lovely and graceful and elegant. She wore lustrous jewels and a shiny satin gown. All their clothing resembled costumes I had seen worn by characters in old films.

I had no idea why looking at these fairy-tale figures and talking about them as they passed through my head got me so excited sexually, but I thought, "What the heck. If this guy doesn't like it, then tough. I'm not going to miss the sensations I'm *experiencing. I'm not going to miss what's happening to me." And the more I talked about the little princess or the queen or the king, the more I felt my vagina just open up. A whole dam of sensual feelings broke loose and I felt like my body was a vagina, from my head to my toes.*

The more I talked, the more orgasms I felt, the more orgasms I wanted, and the more orgasms I was able to have. And it just went on and on. It seemed endless. I didn't want the sex to stop.

I never felt so wonderful in my life, and I thought, "Good Lord! This is what it's all about; this is what it feels like to be a woman." And I was grateful.

Some of you will be surprised at how easy it will be to contact your hidden images during intercourse, the way Charlotte and Harriet were able to in the case histories I've just described. Others will take more time. By accepting and expressing your nonsensual images, and with patience and practice, all of you can learn to develop this skill during sex.

To help you, I've designed some special exercises that will guide you in making your magical journey into *your* past. In order to unearth your sensual treasures, you'll need to learn some simple techniques I call "retracing." These techniques will allow buried memories to resurface from your unconscious and pop onto the TV screen of your mind.

For some the exercises will flow smoothly and effortlessly. That's fine . . . enjoy.

For others, while you may be following each step with great care, it will seem as though nothing is happening. Don't worry . . . this is fine, too. Hang in and keep practicing. Sometimes the unconscious works in strange ways and subliminal processes will be occurring that you won't be aware of. But remember, the mind is never empty. Even when you think the exercises aren't working for you, keep trying and eventually you'll become aware of fleeting glimpses of forgotten childhood memories.

As you continue practicing these retracing exercises, more and more bits of buried information will gradually appear. The ease or the speed with which you find yourself getting results from these exercises has nothing to do with your intelligence or your determination. Regardless of your I.Q. or motivation, many of you may have difficulty at first when attempting to evoke your early images. Don't be discouraged. Your difficulty will be related to a psychological process called . . .

Blocking

Blocking is an unconscious safety device used when you're too frightened to relive an earlier experience which might have been painful, frustrating or very punishing for you. Blocking is like an order sent from your brain, through to your beautiful hidden room, and on to your unconscious mind. It says, "Thou shalt not disturb the repressed material which lies buried here."

When you're blocking, your mind seems to go blank. Sometimes you forget what you were about to say. At other times you suddenly find yourself thinking or talking about a topic that is totally unrelated to the subject you are discussing. This is normal. I encourage patients *not* to ignore this material but to share it with the people they are talking to. It enriches the conversation and creates an atmosphere of trust and camaraderie when you are willing to share a bit of your history that has just popped into your mind. After you say it, you'll probably find that it *is* relevant to the conversation you're involved in.

Here's an example of how old blocked memories can pop into a conversation.

I was working with Colleen in my Monday night group. She was discussing her four-year-old daughter's sex play with a neighbor's child. Jeanne, another group member, interrupted Colleen with some material she had suddenly unblocked from her own childhood:

I just had a flash of my mother pinching my arm so hard, it hurts me now to think about it. We were standing in the hall when it happened. Her face was all snarled up and she was yelling at me for playing doctor in the garage with my cousin.

My stomach is in a knot just thinking about how angry she was with me. I was only four or five years old when it happened, but I had embarrassed her. She said I had let her down—made her feel ashamed. My cousin's mother was very angry with her.

My mom never forgave me for making her look bad in the family—like I was a fallen woman at five! I haven't thought about that for years. I guess I just just blocked away how mean my mother was. I feel so guilty when I remember how cruel she was then, because she's so great to me now.

There is good reason that you block . . . can't remember . . . or may not even want to. As a child, when you were punished for a particular behavior, it was probably made clear to you at that time that whatever you were doing or thinking was "bad." The memory is so painful to you now that you block it out of your mind.

The incident that you don't want to remember may have been something as subtle as a negative glance from a parent, or as frightening as a harsh beating. Everything associated with the incident gets blocked out, as your unconscious goal is to avoid receiving further punishment and feeling frightened, worthless or naughty when you do remember.

Today you may not even recall that original event, but your unconscious does. It remembers everything. While the disapproving glances or beatings from your parents are long since gone, those haunting fears and old anxieties may still be with you.

Through this mechanism of blocking, your unconscious is still trying to protect you from reliving those painful experiences and feeling guilty again.

When practicing your retracing exercises, some of you will find yourselves blocking. In fact, your mind may draw a total blank when you attempt to visualize your early feelings of sensuality. Because they were originally labeled "shameful," "dirty," "perverted," or "bad," you're probably still harboring some unconscious feelings of guilt about them.

In reality, your parents no longer have the same power over you as they had when you were a child. Yet, the impact of those painful lessons still controls much of your present sexual behavior. Sadly, *you're* probably the one now who is continuing to punish *you* for experimental childhood behavior that was perfectly normal and healthy.

Stop clinging to those debilitating and archaic notions. Stop reinforcing the belief that your childhood curiosity and sexual explorations were "bad." You're the adult in charge now. You can go back and positively reevaluate your childhood sexual play. You can change the old negative memories on your early tapes. You can create new tapes with positive new equations.

It's *normal* to want to look, touch, feel and play. It's normal to be curious and experimental. Learn a new equation:

CHILDHOOD SEXUAL PLAY = NORMAL AND
HEALTHY BEHAVIOR.

You can say to yourself, "It's *okay* to remember. I don't have to block out anymore." Now you'll find that it's *good* to go back; it's *necessary* to go back; it's *safe* to go back.

Retracing

There will be different exercises and homework for you to practice as you're learning the PLEASURE PROCESS. In each case read the exercises through several times to yourself to become familiar with them *before* you practice them.

This first exercise should be done when you are alone. It will help you to become totally relaxed so that your mind and your body will be fully receptive. It is in this state that your long-forgotten memories can emerge. When this exercise is finished you will feel very good and very relaxed. Yet, you'll be wide awake and ready for the activities of the rest of your day.

EXERCISE 1: LEARNING TO RELAX DURING RETRACING

Find a quiet, secluded place where you can rest alone, without interruptions. Lie down, get comfortable, and close your eyes.

TAKE A LONG, DEEP BREATH.

Hold this breath for a moment, and at the same time visualize the number 5. Continuing to visualize 5, let your breath go as you silently repeat the word *five* to yourself three times. Go through the same procedure with the number 4, then 3, 2, and 1. Each time remember to:

—Take a deep breath.
—Hold it for a moment as you visualize your number.
—Let your breath out slowly, as you repeat the number to yourself three times, visualizing it as you do this.
—Feel relaxed. Give yourself this peaceful, tranquil space.

You're now ready to instruct your body to move into a state of total relaxation. Starting with your head, concentrate on each part of your body. In a calm, silent voice that only you can hear, tell *all* your muscles to relax and melt away.

PROCEED SLOWLY . . . RELAXING TAKES TIME.
SPEAK SLOWLY TO YOURSELF.

Let all the muscles in your head melt away, as you imagine strong, firm hands gently massaging your scalp. Experience your entire scalp relaxing.

Next, tell the muscles in your eyes to melt away . . . so relaxed . . . feeling so good.
All the muscles in your nose and ears . . . melt away . . . so relaxed.
Let your entire head relax as you fall deeper and deeper into these good feelings.

VERY QUIET . . . VERY CALM,
ENJOY YOUR SWEET, UNIQUE BODY.

Let the screws holding your jawbone together melt away.
Let your mouth hang open slightly.
All the muscles loose and relaxed.
All the muscles in your face . . . forehead . . . all gone . . . melting away.

SO QUIET . . . SO RELAXED.
THINK BACK TO YOUR CHILDHOOD.
LET THOSE EARLY IMAGES AND CHILDHOOD
FANTASIES
BEGIN TO ROAM FREELY IN YOUR HEAD.

Let the muscles in your neck melt away.
Talk silently to them. Tell them to relax.
Imagine gentle, strong hands massaging the back of your neck.
Firm fingers moving along your shoulders . . . massaging . . . feeling so good . . . so relaxed. Let yourself go.
Follow these hands as they go down to massage your back.
Enjoy the feeling of relaxation all over your back.
Relax every muscle.
Talk to every muscle.

ENJOY YOUR BODY.
FEELING SO RESTED . . . SO COMFORTABLE.
CATCH YOUR EROTIC IMAGES FROM
CHILDHOOD.
FOLLOW THEM.

If your images aren't appearing yet . . . that's fine.
Don't worry. They will come later. Just relax and enjoy your sweet body.

Slowly let your arms and hands relax . . . go completely limp.

Let the screws holding your arms and shoulders together melt away.
Relax each muscle in your arms.
Let all the muscles in your hands melt away.
So relaxed.
Talk to each finger separately.
Tell every muscle in your fingers to melt away.

WATCH THE TV SCREEN IN YOUR MIND.
FOLLOW THE IMAGES.

Now talk to your chest.
Tell every muscle to relax.
Take a slow, deep breath.
Fill your lungs with the quiet, peaceful air.
Release your breath slowly as you tell each rib to relax.

SO QUIET . . . SO GOOD.
FALLING DEEPER AND DEEPER INTO THIS
SWEET, RELAXED STATE.

Let all the muscles in your torso relax.
Tell the muscles in your somach to relax, to melt away.

FEELING SO GOOD . . . ENJOYING YOUR
ORIGINAL YOU.
THINK ABOUT HOW NICE IT FEELS TO BE
SENSUAL.

Travel slowly down to your pelvis.
Let all the muscles go.
Relax your buttocks.
Tell every muscle to melt away.

Push down very gently on your anus. Relax.
Let your muscles there melt away.
Let every muscle in your pelvis melt away.
Relax your genitals.

Let your muscles open very slightly.
Let every muscle there melt away.
Enjoy the open, easy feeling.
Let yourself fall deeper and deeper into your body.

SO QUIET . . . SO RELAXED.
THINK ABOUT HOW SENSUAL YOUR BODY IS.
HOW UNIQUE, HOW BEAUTIFUL, HOW SWEET.

Carry on with your legs and feet . . . slowly.
Down through your thighs, knees, calves, ankles, feet and toes.
Tell every part to relax.
Tell all the screws holding your legs and toes together to relax, to melt away.
Imagine now that you're lying on a beautiful, soft mattress made of clouds. Rest comfortably, as you fall deeper and deeper into a quiet, relaxed place.
Let your cloud mattress float high up into the warm sky.
Let the gentle breezes bounce you along.

FEELING SO RELAXED . . . SO SAFE.
LET YOUR MIND ROAM FREELY . . .
BACK TO YOUR EARLIEST SENSUAL MOMENTS.

Let yourself sail away into the warm breezes, as your mind recalls the sensual memories from your childhood.
Let your images flow.
So peaceful, enjoying your sweet ride.
Let your thoughts, as well as your body, float away . . . back . . . way back . . . into your childhood.

Be good to yourself. Allow yourself the time to practice this first exercise daily. It will prove a helpful tool to aid you in the retracing process.

In this next exercise you will begin to release your early sensual images and allow them to surface into awareness. At first, many of your memories may be non-sexual ones. That's fine. Don't disregard them. They are *all* important.

They may appear in disguised form as, say, a flower, a building, or a toy. Perhaps you will see only a flash of a face you knew as a child—your parents, siblings, or a friend. Some of these nonsensual memories will prove later to be sexual.

Go with everything that comes into your mind, as you relax and follow the image. Whether you see something sexual or nonsexual, glimpses of a vague scene or object . . . it doesn't matter. Let yourself be part of the action. Don't censor anything. All of these images are the crucial pieces of your sexual mosaic. They will lead you out of your childhood fear about your sensuality so you can develop a healthy, mature sexual personality.

Lie back and watch your screen. Enjoy your pictures. You are safe here . . . now . . . with your memories.
Remember when . . .

—You peeked through the keyhole and saw your parents undressing? Especially when you caught a glimpse of your mother's breasts or your father's genitals. Wow! That was scary, but so exciting!

—You and your friends played doctor in the garage? You pulled down your pants and so did they. Then your mom caught you. Boy, did you get it. You knew you were doing something terrible by the look on her face.

—You loved to ride on your daddy's foot as though you were astride a horse? It made that nice tingle happen between your legs.

—You loved sliding up and down the banister because the friction felt so good on your genitals?

—You tiptoed to your parents' room late at night when they thought you were asleep? Oh, how you loved to creep up next to the door and listen to that squeaking bed. Your heart was beating so loud you were afraid they'd hear it. It was wonderful hearing those noises, when you rubbed yourself "down there."

—You were so excited seeing your dog lick that long, red thing of his? You just waited for it to go in and out. How disappointed you were when it disappeared into his strange furry tube.

You'll come up with your own collection of images and memories as you learn how to go back and forth between your beautiful hidden room and the present. At first, this exercise will probably be the easiest way for you to go back. But once you know the route, you'll be able to take many spontaneous trips, even without the exercises.

EXERCISE 2: RETRACING DURING NORMAL ACTIVITIES

Your first retracing exercise was designed for you to practice while you were alone and in a secluded place. In this second exercise I want you to teach yourself how to retrace by borrowing some of the relaxation techniques you learned in Exercise 1. *Wherever* you are, *whenever* you have a moment to yourself, you can relax and start the retracing process.

Whether you're waiting in line, stuck in a traffic jam, jogging, bathing, or walking the dogs, you can put yourself into a receptive state and start your retracing. Whatever is happening in your outside world, you can slip away into your thoughts and allow yourself to get in touch with a sensual image from your childhood.

As you continue to practice retracing, images will flow more and more freely. Let them surface. Let them come alive. See how many erotic moments you can recall. Savor them. Invite them to come out and play with you now . . . to roam free and uninhibited.

Each day you'll be more at ease going back and forth between your beautiful hidden room, into the present. It will be fun. Eventually you'll find yourself sharing your images with your mate and even your friends.

EXERCISE 3: YOUR RETRACING NOTEBOOK

It is important to record as many of your old feelings, images and memories as you can. Write them down. When you do, you'll be reinforcing yourself positively. You'll be telling yourself with your adult mind that it was okay then to feel sensual, and it's good now. It's even *better* when you can take that childhood sensuality out of your hidden room and use it today, making it part of your life as a healthy, sexual adult.

Now it's time to find yourself a pen and get ready to start your own erotic notebook. Get used to taking it with you wherever you go. Jot down whatever images you see that flash into your mind.

Get help from the people that were with you when you were small. Ask them questions. Find the missing clues that will help you to remember. Play detective.

—Talk to your parents. See if they can recall any sexual vignettes from your childhood. They may be able to recollect incidents you've forgotten. *Jot them down.*

—Revive old memories by calling on your siblings, friends, and teachers. They, too, may be able to offer sensual remembrances from your past.
Jot them down.

—Rummage through your attic. Help yourself by looking at memorabilia from your childhood: clothes, old report cards, pictures, toys, and so on. Whatever images flash through your mind . . .
Jot them down.

—Look at home movies with your notebook in hand. When forgotten memories break through . . .
Jot them down.

You're organizing a diary of your sexual history. Fill it up; refer back to it; keep adding to it. *Read it.* Your notebook will keep your erotic child alive *now.* Not only are you freeing yourself from the guilt of the past, you're dignifying your healthy sexuality in the present.

Enjoy and respect your sexual history. By using your buried erotica, by bringing it out of your beautiful hidden room, you're organizing a collection of sensual memories that will recharge and revitalize your sexual life today.

Chapter 3

Thou Shalt Not
Relax Down There

*If I worship one thing more than another
it shall be the spread of my own body, or
any part of it.*

—WALT WHITMAN

Not only do your early formative years serve as a training ground for the repression and destruction of your erotic child; it is also during this period that specific physical responses relating to normal genital functioning are repressed. This process occurs in childhood during the initial phases of toilet training.

There was a familiar argument that was popular in the literature on child development in the '30s. It cautioned parents about the damaging potential of punitive toilet training on personality development. But an even more important danger was overlooked: the deleterious effects of a child's associating loss of pelvic control with loss of parental love.

There is too much negative attention paid to the issue of pottie training in many families. Too often after the first year of a child's life, punishment and parental disapproval result when "accidents" occur and the toddler fails to exercise bowel control. Of course, the small child *continually* has accidents and the annoyed parents *continually* issue forth their disapproval.

This leads to an unfortunate paradox. The muscles in the general area of the vagina which control the "on/off" switch for regulating urination and bowel movements are the *same* muscles which play an important role in regulating the "on/off" switch governing multiple orgasms. These are the *sphincter* muscles, which are in the process of maturing during the first two years of life.

When children are little more than six months old, many parents begin nagging them to tighten up these sphincters in order to control their elimination. But this kind of control isn't *physiologically* possible until much later. For example, it isn't until a child is approximately two years old that the sphincter in the anus develops the "grabbing power" it needs to voluntarily close and open as the brain centers command.

The paradox continues to gather strength when you consider that, in order to have good sex, you *must* forget about the controls you were taught as a child concerning your genitals and your body. Adults are overly controlled children who need to be advised on how to relax, loosen up, and let go.

But how can you do this? You've been trained from childhood *not* to lose control. It's been pounded into you for decades that to lose control spells disaster, so by the time you're an adult, the entire concept of letting go and giving up control seems terrifying.

This happens when parents have unrealistic expectation in relation to their children's physical capabilities. They are premature with their toilet-training practices and deliver brutal emotional and sometimes physical punishment. They overteach and overcondition. Because children need their parents' approval, they desperately try to stop making the errors so they can avoid receiving reprimands. In this process, the entire pelvis becomes a focus of anxiety and concern for them.

Finally, after months of premature toilet training, the child comes to fear anything that threatens the control system; for maximum self-protection the child generalizes and decides that *everything* had better be kept locked up down there.

NEVER LOOSEN UP THOSE MUSCLES.
NEVER LOSE CONTROL.

Relaxing the sphincters in any way becomes associated with the fear of being ridiculed and rejected. After repeated trials and daily punishments, the child finally becomes oversaturated with the parents' message and decides:

THOU SHALT NOT RELAX DOWN THERE—
EVER!

We learn our negative lessons too well. We learn to tighten up *all* of our pubic muscles so thoroughly that years later, during sex, we don't know how to reverse the early training; we can't undo the damage and relax the area long enough to allow ourselves to orgasm.

As an adult you probably have little or no memory of this destructive process. But your unconscious fear of your parents' disapproval if you should lose control still hangs on. As you grow up, the memories of the punishments surrounding your bowel training become blurred and forgotten. Yet in situations *unrelated* to eliminating, like having intercourse, many women still can't relax their sphincter muscles and let go. The "thou-shalt-not" lessons have been repeated for too many decades: to lose control spells disaster. As we mature, the pelvic controls during elimination lap over into the pelvic controls during sex. The overlearned message reads:

KEEP YOUR MUSCLES TIGHT.
KEEP THEM CLOSED.
KEEP EVERYTHING IN.

Your toilet training was necessary and vital to your development when you were small. But today it is keeping you from experiencing full sexual pleasure.

You can change. You're an adult now. Toilet training is no longer an important issue for you. You don't need to keep rehearsing those old lessons about sphincter control anymore. You've got it down pat. During sex you can now afford to let your sphincters relax without being concerned about eliminating.

I want to teach you how to relax and use those sphincter muscles. You will feel you've made a *magical* discovery once you've learned how to relax them during sex. This is why I've chosen to call these sphincters your "magical push muscles."

Both men and women have sphincter muscles. However, it is the sphincters in the vagina that are especially important to you as a woman. It is part of the unique physiological packaging that can push you toward unlimited orgasmic responsivity.

If you ask your gynecologist, he or she will probably call your magical push muscle the "pubococcygeus."* During a woman's orgasm, there are involuntary contractions of the push muscles of the vagina. It is important to become familiar with these muscles and to strengthen their tone so that you can produce stronger and more enjoyable orgasms.

---

* Actually what is called the pubococcygeus (your magical push muscle) consists of three parts—the bulbocavernosus, the ischiocavernosus and the pubococcygeus.

It was Dr. Arnold Kegel who first brought attention to the fact that weakness and disuse of these muscles is an important factor in female unresponsiveness. Initially his work was concerned with helping women who were incontinent to improve bladder control by teaching them to increase the strength of their pubococcygeus muscle, which would help them to contain their urine. To do this he developed special exercises for them using an instrument called the *Perineometer*. It enabled his patients to contract and exercise their pubococcygeus muscle against resistance.

Numerous patients began to report that the exercises that were designed to correct the problem of incontinence were inadvertently resulting in an increase of orgasmic responsivity.

Using the information Kegel gathered from his research, the following exercise has been designed to help you move closer toward your multi-orgasmic responses.

EXERCISE 4: GETTING ACQUAINTED WITH YOUR "MAGICAL PUSH MUSCLES"

In the privacy of your bathroom, lock the door and sit down on the toilet. Start to urinate. Then deliberately stop the stream. Hold it for a few seconds, then start to urinate a bit more. Stop again and continue this "urinate—hold—start again—hold—start again" procedure until your bladder is completely empty.

The muscles that enable you to stop and go are your magical push muscles. Become familiar with how it feels to use them—to push in and out on them. Close your eyes as you do this so you can fully concentrate on your body sensations.

Remember how you learned to relax your entire body in an earlier exercise?* Well, muster up these same easy feelings. Spend a few moments sitting on your toilet and telling your entire body to relax before you begin the exercise.

Now push out on your urethra as though you were still trying to force urine to pass. Then relax. Because your bladder is empty, you'll be able to focus solely on the movements of your push muscles.

Push out again and hold your vagina open in this position as long as you can. One of my patients described her sensations at this moment to me:

> When I was doing my exercises on the toilet and I finished with the urinating, I started fantasizing that my opening was a beautiful bulbous flower. When I pushed it out I felt like a lily unfolding and opening up. The longer I kept it open, the more sensual it was. I love to play with myself when my vagina bursts like that. I like touching the fullness and the softness.

Run your finger over the mouth of the opening. Feel the smooth places, the mounds, the valleys. Slip your finger into the opening. Push in and out. Grab your finger with your muscles. Release. Grab again. Notice how the muscles tighten around your finger.

ENJOY THE SENSATIONS.

Keep reminding your body to relax.
Tell your entire pelvis area to relax.
Remove your finger. Place your hand over the outside of your vagina so that it covers the opening of

---

* See Exercise 1 on page 77.

your anus as well. Now push out gently on your anus, as though you were trying to pass wind. Close your eyes and concentrate on these "opening-up" movements. Notice how pushing out on one orifice (the anus) affects the other (the vagina).

Relax all the muscles in the anal area. Then push out slowly again. Try to maintain this easy, open position of your anus for a few seconds. Feel free to grunt a bit. Focus on the sensations of your muscles moving in and out.

Notice how your stomach muscles are moving up and down. This is good. Later on, when you learn how to orgasm more frequently and with strong, deep orgasms, you'll find your stomach muscles will be activated in pleasurable involuntary movements that will almost feel like orgasms themselves.

As you're experiencing the pleasant, gentle movements of your magical push muscles, stomach, and entire pelvis, say to yourself:

I CAN OPEN UP.
I DON'T HAVE TO KEEP IT ALL SHUT DOWN TIGHT ANYMORE.
I CAN LEARN TO RELAX AND LET GO.

You're now starting to reverse the early control procedures you learned as a child. You are experiencing some of the feelings of pelvic release that are the essential prelude to your multi-orgasmic responses.

EXERCISE 5: DAILY PRACTICE WITH YOUR "MAGICAL PUSH MUSCLES"

I recommend that you practice working with your push muscles as often as possible throughout your day. After a while you'll be able to stop worrying about their original function in controlling elimination and you'll be able to concentrate on the pleasurable feelings of their "in and out/opening and closing" sensations.

While telephoning, driving your car, talking, eating, resting, standing in a group or alone, practice your steps. Make this daily practice part of your regular routine:

1. Relax.
2. Push out.
3. Experience the easy, open feelings.
4. Hold for a moment.
5. Relax again.
6. Repeat.

During sex, you will be pushing out on your magical muscles, the same way you did during your exercises. But because you are an adult now and can take care of your eliminating before sex, you will no longer have to worry about maintaining control.

Then all systems are GO!
You're into your senses.
You're into *you*.

By giving up sphincter control during sex, you will intensify your erotic vaginal sensations and pave the way for your orgasms. You will be able to focus completely on your own body. Wherever your partner's body, hands or mouth are, that's where your world will be. Every muscle in your body will be pushing out to receive the sensations.

You will be *all* body, *all* feeling, *totally* aware.

Letting Go

By now you have practiced some of the exercises designed to prepare you for the PLEASURE PROCESS. You have worked on recalling erotic memories from your beautiful hidden room, you have learned to relax, and you have practiced exercises dealing with your magical push muscles. You are learning to remove many sexually inhibiting controls which were developed during childhood. You are learning to let go, both mentally and physically.

You're almost ready to start the PROCESS.

Chapter 4

The Approval Seeker
Within You

*Behold me! I am worthy
Of thy loving, for I love thee!*

——ELIZABETH BARRETT BROWNING

Have you ever been so preoccupied with your thoughts that you've gone way past your exit on the freeway? Or realized that you don't know what has happened during the last five minutes of the television program you are watching?

It's essential to stay in touch with yourself in the "now," the moment things are occurring, because if you don't concentrate on your sensations, important input can slip away unnoticed. This is just as true for nonsexual sensations as it is for sexual sensations.

What do you think about during sex? If you are like most people, you give only a sliver of your attention to your *own* feelings. Much of the time you worry about whether your partner is enjoying what you are doing; you worry about who will climax first, about whether he finds you sensual or attractive. You're so tied up in earning the approval of your partner, so concerned about his wants and needs, that you may be uncomfortable even *thinking* about you.

Why is it so difficult to concentrate on yourself—*your* sensations, *your* feelings, *your* skin? Why can't you just let it all happen and get into the experience? The answers lie in some of the processes involved in your early relationships.

As a child, the search for approval from your parents became an important part of your behavior. For your first four years they were your major source of gratification. You were dependent on them for support and affection. You couldn't survive without them. You quickly learned that the way to receive the most pleasure, the bottom line, was to get mommy's and daddy's approval. You *needed* their approval. They were the only show in town. This need still hovers over you like a dark cloud, long after you have left home to make the break for freedom and independence.

As an adult, you may substitute a lover for your parents (or other authority figures), but you are still driven to please the people who are important to you. You are so busy watching their faces and monitoring their reactions (to make sure you are not displeasing them) that there is little time left for you.

This need for approval is unrelenting. When it surfaces in adult relationships it prohibits optimum sexual functioning. It saps too much of your energy during sex because it forces you to focus on your partner and *forget about you*.

During sex you become a spectator rather than a participant. You become absorbed with interpreting your partner's movements and sounds, to make sure you are doing the "right" thing. You are so intensely involved in earning your partner's approval that you ignore yourself. You are watching, listening, and servicing *his* needs, instead of feeling and enjoying your own.

As a spectator you become a full-time employee in the "pleasing" business, laboring under anxieties like:

—I hope my breath smells okay. I'd better turn my head away, just in case.

—I wonder if he can feel how big my stomach is getting.

—I'll bet I have B.O. I should have taken that shower before we went to bed.

—I'll listen to his breathing to see if he's getting excited.

—I'm afraid he's not getting hard because I'm too fat.

—I'm worried my small breasts are turning him off.

—He isn't kissing me very much tonight. Makes me feel so damn ugly.

—I'd better pretend I'm getting hot or he won't think I'm a passionate woman and he'll leave me.

When your priority is to please, you find yourself thinking, "If my partner is not happy, I must *make* him happy. If my partner is not satisfied, I must *make* him satisfied. If anything goes wrong, it's *all my fault*."

When your priority is to please, you must concentrate on satisfying your partner at the expense of concentrating on your own pleasure. The tragedy is that your own sexual feelings slip away unnoticed. The problem that results is that approval seeking interferes with having good sex. The dilemma—or "double bind" —looks like this: to be labeled a *good* child, you must learn to be an approval seeker. But:

approval seeking makes good sex impossible.

The more important your partner is to you, the more you slave for his approval. In fact, you feel so needy and dependent that you don't realize your mate is feeling the same way: he needs *your* approval. He is afraid *you're* the one who's going to be rejecting.

What *neither* of you realizes is that you both run equal risks. Emotionally, you're in the same boat. You're both needy and dependent.

You live in fear.

You dread being criticized or rejected by your lover, so you attempt to avoid this possibility by becoming an approval seeker. You forget your own wants and needs.

Each woman I've treated stops herself in her own way. At cocktail parties she holds back her comments and questions because she thinks they're foolish, not important, uninteresting. She fears that if she presents herself and speaks, then everyone there will know how stupid she is. She is silent. "I know I'm not smart enough. My ideas aren't worth hearing, so I hold back because by exposing myself, I'll be ridiculed."

As small children we learn that by being silent, by stopping and withdrawing into ourselves, we get hurt less, we avoid punishment. This notion of stopping ourselves transfers into our adult sexuality. Many patients report that they hold back sensual feelings for similar reasons. "He'll think there's something wrong with me, that my way—what I need or want—is whorey, oversexed, peculiar."

With all the women I've worked with, the methods used for blotting out the slightest show of sensuality are as different as their individual histories, yet very much the same in their underlying theme. Each woman slaps her own hand emotionally when she is in bed and quiets the voice that talks to her, the sensual voice she's afraid will surface and cause her to be censured.

After a while you wind up abandoning your own body and your own sensuality. You may even feel guilty when you focus on yourself because you're afraid you may be neglecting your partner. In the end you may even feel guilty about experiencing any pleasure at all!

This kind of self-destructive thinking results in a firmly implanted belief: *when you're in love you must forget about yourself and devote yourself to your partner's needs.*

So you lose out! No pleasure for you because you unconsciously decide that you must always take good care of your partner and ignore *you.*

You may, however, allow yourself one exception: when you're *not* in love, and your partner *isn't* very important to you and you're *not* very interested in his approval, then you feel free to please *yourself.* In other words, you can enjoy good sex only in casual encounters.

Here's a case history that points out how we rob ourselves of feeling sensual when we're worried about our partner's approval.

MILLIE'S BLACK STOCKINGS

Millie had met her husband Harry at a neighborhood street party in Brooklyn. It was "love at first sight." Two weeks after the party they ran off and got married.

Millie was finishing high school and Harry was a traveling salesman working for a cosmetics company. He was twenty-six and had experienced sex with several other persons. Millie was only seventeen. Although she had necked and petted since she was thirteen, she was still a virgin when they got married.

Millie and Harry had been together for six years when she came in to see me. She was concerned that their sex life had come to a near standstill.

Millie had begun masturbating when she was fifteen. She had developed a favorite ritual. Every Saturday night her parents went out and she was left to babysit with her younger brother. As soon as he was asleep she would turn on her favorite music and strip. Leaving her top bare, she would put on her mother's black stockings and high heels and dance in front of the mirror.

Millie had beautiful long legs and she loved watching herself. As she danced her hands would caress her body. Eventually they would find their way down to her vagina. She would always get very excited seeing herself in the mirror when she masturbated. She usually enjoyed two or three orgasms before the dance was over.

During the first two years of Millie's marriage Harry was on the road about four days a week. When he came home they were so happy together and so in love that they had sex almost every day. Millie seemed to enjoy their lovemaking, but she never had an orgasm. However, when Harry was out of town, she would don her black stockings and masturbate before the mirror the way she had before they were married. Only then could she have orgasms.

Millie never told Harry about her dance/masturbation ritual. She was worried he *wouldn't approve* because she once overheard him comment to a friend that he was certain masturbation was rare among married couples.

Another incident that convinced her that Harry would disapprove occurred one night when they were dressing to go out to a party. Millie wore a black suit and put on black hose. Harry looked at her as they were ready to leave and said, "Honey, those black stockings look so whorey. Put on the pale beige ones you usually wear. Your legs look so gorgeous in them." And while that was the last time Millie wore black stockings in front of Harry, she nonetheless continued her secretive masturbation dance when he was gone.

Months later Millie started having an affair with the

doorman in their building. It happened one night when she was out taking a walk. Harry was on the road. Millie had put on her black suit with the black stockings and decided to take a stroll before going to sleep. The doorman was a young college student who worked nights at their apartment building. She had never paid much attention to him. But that night he was so charming and attentive in his praise of her "sexy, beautiful legs" that she sat down in the lobby and visited with him. He started stroking her legs and talking about what a "turn-on" she was. A few minutes later they were upstairs in her apartment listening to music and drinking wine.

The doorman asked Millie to pick up her dress a little and pose for him in front of the mirror. He caressed and petted her body as she started swaying to the music. She didn't know him very well and couldn't have cared less whether he thought her hose were whorey. Millie didn't care if he approved or not, because he didn't matter. She almost tuned him out as she enjoyed looking at her legs and dancing in his arms. She was totally into her own feelings and sensations.

That night they had sex and Millie orgasmed for the first time with a man. It was the beginning of several extramarital episodes with casual acquaintances and strangers. It was always the same: she'd wear her black stockings, feel free to enjoy herself without worrying about her partner, and every time she would orgasm.

Millie's guilt feelings about her extramarital affairs began to depress her, and she decided to come in for therapy. After several months of encouragement and support, she finally dared to risk Harry's disapproval. One night while they were watching television, Millie slipped away into the bedroom. A few minutes later she came out dancing. She was nude—except for her high heels and black stockings.

At first, Harry looked surprised. But within minutes

they were making love on the living room carpet. Millie orgasmed with Harry for the first time in their marriage.

Afterwards Millie said, "I thought you didn't like me in black stockings. You thought they looked whorey."

"They do look whorey," said Harry. "I don't want you out in the street looking like that, but I love it here in the living room, baby." From that moment on black stockings became a delightful part of their sexual repertoire.

Millie discovered that by not worrying about her husband's approval she was able to do what turned *her* on. She became so passionate, it was infectious; her husband became aroused, too.

When you can accept and approve of yourself as a person who has highly specific needs and wants in sex, then you can be concerned with yourself, even when you're with a partner you love. You'll be able to change the sad equations that came out of your childhood, when you were afraid that any disapproval would result in being abandoned. You can stop worrying now because: you're grown up; you're old enough to take care of yourself; you can learn to be the source of your own approval.

You can stop worrying about your partner's negative judgments and criticism. You can learn to change your obsolete equations, be more aware of your own sexual desires and preferences. You can allow yourself to be more spontaneous and creative during sex. And this can all happen when you *are* involved and you *are* in love.

Practice this new equation. Say it out loud to yourself several times a day:

Great love and involvement = Little need for approval.
It's okay to take care of myself and do what I want!

The Smoke Screen of the Approval Seeker

Most of us are experts at delivering approval-seeking messages. We practice them daily. Typically, we're un-aware we're using them. They appear in our speech and thinking, distorting the real meaning of our messages and confusing our partners. They are misleading.

The approval seeker unwittingly disguises the mes-sage, so that the receiver never actually knows what is happening. She sounds like this:

"You are the best sex partner I've ever had."

(when the truth is . . .)

"You're one of the lousiest lovers I've ever had. You never seem to know what to do with my body. I'll never tell you because I'm afraid it will hurt or discourage you. Then we'll never have any sex and that'll kill our marriage."

Stop withholding!

By withholding information about your body—what feels good, what excites you—sex probably will become so dull for both of you, it *will* be intolerable. And that *will* kill your marriage!

When you use approval-seeking messages, you are holding back the important ideas and feelings about your sexuality that your partner needs to know: the gestures and responses that frighten you, turn you off, hurt or worry you. You hide these feelings, so your partner assumes that you are happy and satisfied be-cause of all the approval you're sending out. No reality . . . just approval.

Regardless of his efforts, effectiveness or behavior, your feedback is always the same. There are no *consequences* to his behavior: if sex is awful, you deliver approval; if sex is wonderful, you deliver approval.

No one can change or improve or respond effectively under the blinding smoke screen of the approval seeker, because *no one can tell what is really going on.* No one knows what to do, or what *not* to do. Communication stops; behavior can't be altered; sex doesn't improve.

Your mate needs to know what the problems are and what he can do about them. But when you begin to communicate and to discuss problems, you'll need to be careful. Your mate will be able to listen only when you deliver messages that are *full* of positives and *free* of blame, criticism or guilt. Remember, your mate is an approval seeker too.

When you can be positive, *honestly* positive, he will be able to hang in and listen. Remind him of all the good things you enjoy about your sex. Don't forget to include the subtle nuances and shadings, the little things he does that you cherish. But remember: the information can't be received and processed unless it is accompanied by large amounts of honest positives.

If you're thinking, "Why so much caution? Why do I need to be so careful?" it's because *your* partner, and everyone else's partner, feels very fragile and very little. *So tread softly.*

It is important to:

LET YOUR PARTNER KNOW WHAT'S REALLY
HAPPENING TO YOU.

—Don't withhold important wants and feelings about the things you enjoy (the way Millie did). *Don't hide.*

—Don't withhold the important feedback he'll need in order to understand you sexually. Tell your partner if any of his gestures or responses frightens you. Tell him about the things that turn you off, and the disappointments that hurt or worry you. But when you do, always start out by mentioning the positive feelings you're enjoying first.

We are all children inside, and a barrage of pure criticism or blame is just too tough to process. No one can listen to totally negative information about himself.

No one is big enough to handle feeling "bad" or inadequate. The approval seeker's ears close shut with the slightest threat of criticism. And this criticism not only hurts, but often immobilizes behavior (the reverse of what you're seeking).

Both partners can deal with, and profit by, negative information, providing these negatives come in small bits, generously surrounded by plenty of positives, and providing these bits do not suggest that anyone has been deliberately hurtful or has intentionally done something wrong.

Guilty people *cannot* change—so no *blaming*. A pure negative delivery of "Why can't you ever do that" or "I hate this about our sex" will result in anger and distancing. Your partner will appear uninterested, and sexual activity will come to a halt.

Rather, make certain your sexual wants, needs and expectations are presented in small doses, wrapped in the happy, positive memories you've shared together. When you can add lots of positives to your communications, you can then afford to include some short, carefully placed wants, directions and negatives such as:

Example #1

Positive: I feel so good.

Positive: I'm having so much fun.

Positive: My whole body is tingling.

Direction: I think it would feel good to . . .

Positive: I'm having so much fun. (Repeat of any positive is fine.)

Note how the "direction" was surrounded by positives.

Example #2

Positive: I love the way you kiss my breasts.

Positive: It really gets me hot.

Positive: Every time you play with them it feels good in my vagina.

Negative: Honey, I don't want you to bite so hard.

Positive: I love the way my vagina swells when you kiss my breasts.

Note how the "negative" was surrounded by positives.

You may want to make other comments such as: "I'd like to try this . . . I think it would be fun to . . . I get frightened when you . . . I want you to . . . It worries me if . . . I don't enjoy the. . . ." But be sure you wrap all of your wants, directions and negatives within a generous blanket of honest positives

Don't assure your partner that you are happy and satisfied when it isn't true; *don't pretend* to be in ecstasy when you can't wait until he dismounts. And above all, *don't feign* orgasm or there isn't a chance for you to learn how to be a happy and healthy person sexually.

Your sex life can improve only when your mate knows what the problems are. Talk to him warmly, affectionately and openly. In my practice I've found that over 90 percent of the sexual problems I encounter can be worked out when each partner is aware of what's really happening to the other.

Too often in a sexual relationship with someone you love, communication tends to break down. This can happen when the approval seeker's smoke screen of unqualified positive feedback becomes so confusing that neither partner knows what the other is experiencing.

But remember, communication *also* tends to break down (as does the sex) if the feedback is all negative. No one has the ego strength to handle a steady barrage of criticism.

Pure Criticism Can Be Immobilizing

Criticism not only hurts, but can be immobilizing. The fear of failure can be so painful, sometimes it's easier not to have sex at all.

Both partners can profit from negative feedback, *providing* the negative information is given in a loving, supportive way. Present your negatives in small bits, generously salted with plenty of positives. Be sure to include everything you can about what your partner does that you really *do like*.

Here are some examples:

Negatives	Positives
Criticism like this will hurt:	This message will result in positive change:
"Why are you biting my nipples? Don't you know that hurts, damn it?"	"I'm so turned on by how soft your lips are. Don't bite, love; your lips are wonderful."

Negatives	*Positives*
"Why am I always the one who has to run after you to start sex? You're not helpless! Why don't you get things going once in a while?"	"It was so sweet the way you started rubbing my back last night. It really got things going. I felt so excited when you were so loving and came on to me."
"It drives me crazy when you go for my vagina the minute we hit the bed."	"I love the way your hands feel on my body. They're so soft and gentle. Yet, sometimes I get frightened when you reach for my vagina too quickly.
	"I felt so safe last week when you held me for a while and played with my breasts first."

When you learn to express your sexual feelings honestly, without misleading approval-seeking messages and without damaging negative criticism, you're on the road toward achieving realistic and positive sexual communication.

Chapter 5

The Real You—
Being an Original

*To be nobody but yourself in a world
which is doing its best night and day to
make you everybody else, means to fight
the hardest battle which any human being
can fight, and never stop fighting.*

—E. E. CUMMINGS

There are two advantages to overcoming approval-seeking behavior. We have already discussed one: honest communication. The other is that you can learn to be yourself by finding approval from *within* yourself. Instead of being who you think others want you to be, you can be who you *are,* who you want to be—the "real" you.

Don't lose sight of who you really are. When you abandon your real identity, you lose your true self. When you live by someone else's standards, you betray your own.

Don't listen to the media. They are hawking a sterile brand of "sexola" which is being packaged for you much like a breakfast cereal. They're selling sexual fantasies, formulas and recipes that are mass-designed and have nothing to do with your erotic history. Madison Avenue doesn't know what's in your beautiful hidden room—*only you do.* But the call of their sirens is so loud and their promises are so seductive that you buy them . . . and end up feeling empty and inadequate . . . a hard-core imitator of love, feigning emotions and waiting for that hollow orgasm. It's a dehumanizing trap.

Get in touch with your own brand of sensuality. It's time to stop pretending you're in someone else's body, wearing someone else's soul, designed for someone else's life.

Take a chance on your authentic personality. Don't feign your sexual signature. There's another original out there who's going to want you just as you are.

There has never been anyone quite like you, and there never will be because *you are special*.

You have the power to make the most of what you are. Regardless of your size, shape, weight or gait. Score your assets and count your positives. There are people out there who will appreciate *your* kind of beauty.

Learn to take advantage of what you have, because beauty is a state of mind. It is an inner feeling, a spiritual condition.

There is beauty in the grace with which you accept your flaws. There is beauty in your appearance. There is beauty in the true fabric of your character. But, ultimately, this all boils down to the beauty of your *originality*. No one else can duplicate the uniqueness that is yours.

Embrace your authentic self. Discover your own inner sense of you. Present who you really are, because following someone else's formula and pretending to be someone you're not can be disastrous.

CYNTHIA'S PRETENDING

The importance of presenting who you are was demonstrated to me in the case history of a patient named Cynthia. During her entire first session Cynthia was crying. She explained that her boyfriend, Hank, had just left her, after they'd lived together for only two months.

> I was so impressed with him when we first met that I couldn't believe he liked me. He was the best-looking man in the store where I worked. I was so flattered that I was on guard every minute, pretending to be all the things he told me that he loved about a woman.

> He said he enjoyed classical music, so I said I did too, even though I hate it. He said his favorite food was shrimp, full of garlic—and I said that was my favorite food, too. I kept pretending because I wanted him to love me and to think we had a lot in common.

> After two months of living together I started slipping and the real me began creeping out. I think when he got a look at the person I really am, instead of the one I was attempting to be all these months, he left me.

It's too costly to pretend and be rejected later. It's much less painful to *present you* from the beginning, knowing that either you'll make it or you won't—the relationship will grow and become better or you'll lose it on the first night. Being rejected after you've invested a lot of yourself hurts too much; it pays in the long run to be the real, authentic you.

Falling in Love with You

It takes *two real people* to have a good relationship; one of them must be *you*. And the first step toward loving someone else is falling in love with you. Herein lies the touchstone to real personal security and dignity.

Like you, most people feel uncertain and vulnerable much of the time. Everyone is convinced that the next person is smarter, more attractive, more clever in business, a wiser parent, and a better lover. It's time for you to realize that everyone else out there probably feels just as inadequate and self-critical as you do.

The *San Francisco Examiner,* in a study conducted in 1977, discovered that 80 percent of the people interviewed believed that other people were more attractive, had a better sex life, and had more fun than they did.

In my own practice I've found that the beautiful model is ashamed of the stretch marks on her stomach; the 25-year-old film star is worried she's a bore off-screen; the millionaire is afraid no one really likes him for himself; the football hero is concerned that he's not educated. We're all in the same boat, so stop comparing yourself negatively.

Accept your imperfections and scars of living. Everyone has them. Without them you would not be human or interesting.

The man you have sex with is just going to be a human being. There's nothing else out there. And he's going to be worrying about things like his penis being too small, his hair falling out, and his stomach getting too big. He's not going to be analyzing your stretch marks or the pimple at the back of your neck. He won't have time. He'll be so busy wondering if he's going to get it up or if you're going to like him or if *his* breath smells, he won't have time to analyze or criticize you.

No one is as interested in criticizing, helping or training you as your parents were. They had a lot at stake in your formative years in getting you into school looking and behaving like an appropriate little human being. But the man you're going to be going to bed with is too busy worrying and swimming upstream himself. He's not going to have time to analyze your flaws. He's going to be too busy wondering if you're analyzing his.

Every man has highly individualized preferences relating to the female anatomy, based on his personal erotic history. If you are involved with a man who was originally attracted to your big breasts and ample thighs, and you decide to join the "Pepsi generation" and become slim and trim, you'll probably turn him off. There is a reason he selected you, and the reason lies buried in *his* beautiful hidden room.

Few of the men you will encounter had mothers who were great beauties or film stars. Their first sensual experiences were associated with women who were oversized or undersized in some way. And their contemporary ability to become aroused is linked to these early erotic associations.

If your breasts are a 32 (or a 42) there will be someone out there who will love them just the way they are. He'll probably be the fellow whose mother had small boobs and big hips—or the reverse. Perhaps the first woman he ever felt an erection with was shaped just like you. Attraction and chemistry have very little to do with reality. They are mostly based on old experiences and connections and old neurotic interactions.

So stop worrying about what you think are your weaknesses and shortcomings—he may have selected you because of them! Accept *your* originality . . . *your* humanness. Learn how to say to your love, "Here I am. Accept me and love me, with all my flaws, confusion and fears. I want to share my precious moments with you."

EXERCISE 6: DEVELOPING SELF-AWARENESS AND SELF-ACCEPTANCE

This exercise is designed to teach you to appreciate and approve of yourself *as you are*. It's critical in the PLEASURE PROCESS to gain self-awareness and self-acceptance so that you are not dependent upon your partner's approval. Then, during sex, whatever you're feeling at the moment can become your total world. You will no longer let your concerns revolve around your imperfections. By learning to *center* your awareness on *yourself,* and by accepting your body and your uniqueness, you will be able to experience your sexuality more fully.

The exercise will help you to remove yourself from negative thoughts and intruding anxieties of your nonsexual life, and help you to move into the feelings and joy of your sexual world. It comes from my studies in Eastern philosophy, Yoga, and Zen. When you use these chantlike phrases, substitute your name and your roles for mine. Repeat these words aloud when you're alone, until they eventually become an automatic part of your thinking processes while you're having sex.

I am Irene Kassorla.

Although I am a mother, daughter, citizen, homemaker, psychologist—none of these things is important to me at this moment.

Right now, I am a sensual and responsive human being . . .

A unique and original *me*.

I have a body, but I am not my body; I am more.

My stretch marks, scars, wrinkles testify to my strength and courage in living and surviving.

I am a beautiful and original *me*.

I have many negative memories from my past, but now I can put these old disappointments, frustrations and resentments to rest.

I can allow myself to feel love, tenderness, and excitement.

I can be happy.

I am a beautiful and original *me*.

I have goals, but right now I am not my goals.

They are not me.

Now I do not desire prestige and approval.

I desire to be caressed, stroked, and petted.

I have an intellect, but I am not my intellect.

It is not me.

I am a therapist. I cure and help. But not now . . . not in bed.

Here I am a child in an erotic playground: laughing, sharing, crying, having fun, singing, talking, loving, orgasming . . .

Feeling womanly and sensual.

What am I, then?

What remains after discarding my flaws, my roles, my negative history, my goals, and the outside world?

I am my own center of awareness and passions.

I am the full, experiencing me . . .

The beautiful and original me.

I am capable of mastering and concentrating all of
my psychological processes and my total physical
being on my sexuality . . . in this moment . . . *now!*

EXERCISE 7: GETTING ACQUAINTED WITH YOU

This exercise is designed to help you get acquainted
with your original you. This is another step in gaining
more awareness and self-acceptance. As in Exercise 6,
you will learn to center your awareness on yourself and
enjoy the sensuality of your uniqueness.

The objective in this exercise is to hug, examine,
caress and gently touch each part of your body as you
get acquainted with *you*.

Find a quiet time to lie down on your bed and relax,
alone and unclothed. See to it that you have complete
privacy, without outside noises to divert your thoughts.
Close your eyes. Then . . .

Begin to explore your body.

Start with your face and slowly run your fingers over
your forehead.

Relax.

Enjoy.

Explore the ins and outs, the hard and soft places,
where the contours are round or angular, where the
hair meets the skin, the bony spots, the openings. Move
slowly. Examine every detail—every part. Let your
fingers be your silent guide leading you from place to
place.

Slowly, gently, move down your body.

Relax.

Enjoy.

Think about how wonderful your body is—the efficiency of all your healthy parts. How accurately everything works: how easily your limbs change position, your eyes see, your ears hear, your brain thinks, your mouth speaks.

Your body is a miracle of human engineering.

How perfect your erotic areas are. They are located in just the right places, move and function with such precision.

Experience the miracle of your body.

Get acquainted with yourself.

Relax.

Enjoy.

Touch your breasts, feel their softness, roundness. Examine your nipples. See how hard they become as you fondle them. Be tender. Feel the soft hair covering your pubis. Touch the lips of your vagina. Examine the ins, the outs, the soft and hard places.

Gently caress your sweet body.

Hug yourself.

Relax.

Enjoy.

Run your fingers along your arms. Feel the bony places, the muscles, the veins. Trace the ribs on your torso. Feel your navel. Run your hands over your stomach. Feel your hips, your thighs and the rest of your legs.

Explore your healthy body.

Relax.

Enjoy.

Say to yourself: "This is good, this is fun, this is normal, this is healthy. I feel so feminine. I feel so lovely."

Trace the outline of your body as you move on to each new part—touching, examining, enjoying every sensation, stimulating every nerve ending. Proceed slowly so you can savor the moment.

Revel in the wonder of your

UNIQUENESS and ORIGINALITY.

EXERCISE 8: ALTERING THE CONDITIONS

Once you're able to feel comfortable going through Exercise 7, I want you to repeat the steps under slightly different conditions. This will allow you additional ways in which to appreciate and experience yourself.

Try out these new conditions:

—Instead of lying in bed, try practicing the exercise while soaking in a warm, scented bubble bath.

—For another variation on the theme, rub your body with oil as you go through the steps.

—Apply heat (using a heating pad) and cold (using ice cubes) on your skin alternately as you go through the steps; this will heighten the sensitivity of the receptors in your skin.

—Use a string of beads, or something soft such as a fur muff or a chiffon scarf, to trace gently over your body as you go through the steps of the exercise.

You will discover other ways to experience your body and to get in touch with your sensuality. Each new vehicle will enable you to expand your awareness, self-appreciation and self-acceptance. Then your compelling need to seek approval during sex can diminish. By approving of yourself, you will be able to experiment with your sexuality more completely, becoming more spontaneous and inventive.

Now, in the PLEASURE PROCESS, you will learn to concentrate more on your own sensations. You will discover all the excitement that your healthy body has waiting for you.

PART TWO:

THE
PLEASURE
PROCESS

Chapter 6

Prelude
to the Process

*If anything comes naturally to man
without any prior learning and experience,
it is not sexual intercourse.*

—ALBERT ELLIS

Stop for a moment now and imagine being a free, spontaneous and completely happy person during sex. Imagine learning how to achieve total sexual satisfaction in a loving way every time you want to. This is all possible for you in the PLEASURE PROCESS as you start learning how to concentrate on *you*.

While you are caring, kind and loving to your partner, you're not thinking about *his* needs. Rather, you're zeroing in on your *own* pleasurable sensations. You are convinced you deserve it. *You're worth it*.

You are in the process of learning the best ways to recognize and appreciate your own originality and expand your joyful limits. By falling into your own special world of erotica, you will better be able to share a sensual playmate with your partner . . . *you!*

You and your partner can learn in this PROCESS to understand each other's sexual preferences, prejudices, and points of view, so conflicts can be terminated quickly. You'll be able to enjoy the long hours of pleas-

123

ant verbal exchanges, offering information about what you think, need, and want sexually. Differences can be discussed and resolved by compromise because the person who learns to be happy in sex can become a good problem solver, not a fighter and not a worrier.

Under the carefully structured guidance of the PLEASURE PROCESS, your ego will have an opportunity to expand and flourish. Pleasurable sex is one of the easiest ways in life to achieve great measures of pride, success and feelings of power in the sanctity of your personal happiness.

Practice Makes Perfect

John Ruskin said, "When love and skill work together; expect a masterpiece." Practice *does* make perfect, especially in sex. Like any other human activity, sex is a skill that has to be learned, practiced, and honed to precision. Of course, when it comes to sex, we've been indoctrinated to believe that only someone who trades in sex and makes a living out of it would want to make a skill of it. "Nice people" aren't supposed to know much, do much, think or enjoy much about sex. It's all instinctive, anyway . . . you just let it happen.

Nonsense! Why take the risk of ignoring helpful information and just let it happen? With that kind of laissez-faire philosophy, it usually happens infrequently and badly.

You've already seen that the ignorance and unwillingness to learn about your sensuality came from the unknowns and the dark fears from your past. For years you have stored these fears and unknowns in your beautiful hidden room, not realizing that waiting behind that door lay not a demon, but rather an innocent and precious child. This is the same erotic child who can teach you the unique mysteries and magic of your sexual self. It is when you can welcome, embrace and accept the erotic child within you that you will be able to free your treasure lode of sensuality.

Before the Music Starts

I want to introduce you to the techniques that you'll be learning in the PLEASURE PROCESS, but before I do, I'd like to explain a little bit about the philosophy.

The importance of foreplay has been emphasized ad nauseum by most books and magazines concerned with educating the public on sex. While it is true that foreplay is the most important physical preparation for intercourse, there is an even more important area that has been too often neglected in sexual education. It is the *mental* and *emotional* preparation for good sex.

I'm concerned with how quickly lovers start moving into intercourse without sufficient mental and emotional preparation. Almost as soon as they touch each other, the man's hand is down on the vagina doing what he's heard is called "foreplay." That is, he starts grinding away at the vagina almost the minute physical contact is made.

Now while it might be possible to find a woman who can lubricate instantly, it's so rare that I want to forget about that woman and talk about "most women." Most women tend to lubricate slowly and enjoy moving into sex at a gradual pace. They find it repulsive and a turn-off to be hurried. So one of the most intrusive and negative things a man can do is to move his hand almost immediately down to the vagina and start what I call the "vaginal grind." It is a technique that may be ideal for creating a sore vagina or removing skin, but it has *nothing* to do with sexual excitement!

When a man reaches too quickly for your vagina and it's dry—which it will be unless you're Superwoman or very unusual—if you're like most women, you find it very discouraging. You probably feel inadequate. You may think to yourself, "Well, if he's putting his hand down there already, that means I *should* be lubricating. And if I'm not lubricating, then there's got to be something very wrong with me."

A man experiences similar feelings when he is impotent and a woman reaches down and finds his soft, mushy mass. That can be very discouraging to him if he thinks that his masculinity is dependent upon a constantly erect and turgid hard-on.

This is true for women as well. Many women feel that their femininity is measured by an instantly swollen, wet and juicy vagina. And when it isn't—they feel discouraged.

Before Foreplay

The slow-motion cadence of the PLEASURE PROCESS allows you to slip into an aura of peacefulness and safety that serves to heighten the intensity of what you'll be able to experience, while at the same time eliminating the nagging fear of feeling inadequate or of failing. Therefore not only will we be thinking in terms of foreplay, but we'll focus on slowing up even more in "Before Foreplay."

You may be worrying now because you're afraid that your husband or lover is going to say, "Slow up intercourse even more!! That sounds awful. I don't want to hang around and wait forever. I thought this was supposed to be more fun."* If he does, you can honestly tell him he's *right*. Because the whole idea of the PLEASURE PROCESS is to guarantee more fun for *both* of you—and certainly for *him*. He won't believe this yet, but not only will he be getting a much more passionate, interested and involved woman, he will be having more erections than he *or* you ever thought possible.

Many of my patients report that while they're working on the PROCESS, their husbands, who formerly would have one or perhaps two orgasms during a single episode of lovemaking, are now capable of having four or five erections.

When a man sees his woman becoming so incredibly sensual right before his eyes, when he realizes that he is the orchestrator of all this sensual music, this gives him such a sense of pride and power that experiencing more erections than he is used to is not unusual. Many men feel that for them, this is the true added bonus of the PLEASURE PROCESS.

The Physiological Dilemma

There is a real physiological dilemma in sex that needs to be dealt with. Physiologically most men can achieve instant orgasm, whereas the vagina, because women tend to be "head oriented" and less genitally oriented, may need as much as an hour to get ready.

---

* If your husband or lover argues that he can't wait very long because he's afraid it will damage him physiologically—the old myth of the "blue balls"—assure him this is nonsense. According to Dr. Richard Bank, the noted gynecological expert and surgeon, "Sexual excitation without the accompanying gratification caused by orgasm and ejaculation may produce transient pelvic discomfort due to penis congestion but this is a *harmless,* self-limiting, absolutely benign condition which is short-lived and which carries no complications or sequeli whatsoever."

There's instant tea and there is instant coffee, but instant sexual excitement in women is very unusual. Kinsey noted that so many women are adversely conditioned to sexual stimulation that they require an unreasonable length of time to reach orgasm.

It's a whole package with a woman. By the time she works her way through feeling "safe" and wondering "is he going to use me," and "does he really care about me," or "does he just want to get it off"—and the rest of her "ands," "if only's" and "buts," not to mention her early history—she's exhausted. She's not even interested anymore.

> *The vagina doesn't really start getting wet*
> *until the head feels good.*

AREN'T YOU READY YET?

That's what my patient Bernie always said as he was grinding away at his wife's clitoris. In their therapy session together Dee, Bernie's wife, explained:

> *I used to like to have sex before we were married, because we did so much hugging and petting in the car, beforehand. By the time we would find a place to have sex—which we had to sneak in before my parents got home or when Bernie's parents were out of town—we were both so hot that neither of us could wait.*

> *Now, since we've been married, I'm hardly ever in the mood because there's so little satisfaction for me. It all goes so fast. The minute we get into the bedroom, Bernie already has a hard-on. I just know there's no way I can compete with him and make it to orgasm. He's ready before I even get*

my pants off. I get so discouraged realizing that he's already panting heavily and I'm not even thinking, yet, about sex. I can't win. Bernie already has a mile head start and my vagina is absolutely dry.

When we get in bed and he immediately grabs for my crotch, I get such a sense of failure that I'm totally turned off. I'm absolutely cold. I don't want to get into a race with Bernie because I know there's no way in the world I'm going to win. He's going to rub my vagina for three seconds; he's going to kiss my breasts for another three seconds; then he's going to throw it in, stroke three times, and come.

Who needs it? Why should I watch him come? I'd rather say I'm tired from all the housework and being with the kids all day. Otherwise, before I know it he's turned over and he's sleeping. And I'm left lying there with a vagina full of sperm, hating him and myself.

How can a woman possibly relax under this kind of pressure to perform? She can't. She needs to be cuddled, she needs to feel cared for . . . to know that there is hope for her to share equally in the pleasurable feelings *and* the orgasm.

Stop the Negative Camera!

Once your partner learns to slow up and better understands the techniques that will be outlined in the PLEASURE PROCESS, you'll have time to turn your attention to yourself and look at the problems *you* may be encouraging. Common among these is the tendency many people have—both men and women—to unwittingly introduce old negative associations and arguments into the bedroom.

Your mind is much like a movie camera in that various scenes are continually playing their themes in your head. This is your thinking process, but when it is negative, it destroys any ongoing pleasure that might be available to you. Being negative is a consuming, all-encompassing occupation that will take up all of your thinking time. You'll be so preoccupied that there won't be any time for fun, or any time to get in touch with pleasure. And in order to enjoy yourself in your adult sexual life, it is necessary to stop these negatives and fill your head with positives.

Whenever my patients are thinking something that is self-destructive or that stops them from enjoying their sex or their lives in some way (like old stored-up resentments, unresolved fights and bitter, lingering hatreds), I explain to them that they can get these corrosive thoughts out of their minds by a process I call "Stop the Negative Camera."

I want to help *you* learn to stop *your* negative camera. This camera starts rolling when you're feeling sexual and stops you by winding back to all the old propaganda that you were originally fed about sex— that it is dirty and sinful. These tapes are filled with the negative, guilt-laden messages that you've been playing and replaying for years. These are the *conscious* thoughts you've been using to convince yourself that your sexual feelings or longings are wrong. These are the thoughts that were implanted in your head when you were small. It was then that you absorbed all sorts of negative pictures about sex which were really part of your parents' value systems.

Now that you're an adult you may want to eliminate

some of these tapes. The "goods" and "bads" that your parents felt were appropriate decades ago may not be your "goods" and "bads" today. Now you have a chance, as an adult, to go through a filtering-out process and remove some of these negative pictures. This can be done according to *your* present value system, *your* own preferences and designs—and using *your* *adult head.*

You can go back now and erase some of the negative scenes that are hindering you today and destroying some of the fun in your sex life. For example, say that your husband is starting to hug and caress you and suddenly you find yourself freezing up, thinking, "I don't feel like having sex now. I'm just not in the mood. I'm not interested. Why does he always come at me like this? I wish he'd leave me alone."

My experience has been that these feelings are related to old remnants of the tapes that your parents repeatedly played to you about the "nos," "don'ts," and all the rest of the FORBIDDENS. So when your boyfriend, husband or lover starts caressing you, the FORBIDDEN sign goes up and your negative camera starts playing. All the old "wrongs," "bads" and "don'ts" you learned in relation to pleasure and genitals start rolling.

Remember when you were six and told your mommy that you and the little boy next door pulled down your pants and touched each other between your legs? Remember how your mother had that horrified look on her face? Today, when you say you're not in the mood or you're too tired or you have a headache, you're probably unconsciously trying to avoid replaying mother's horrified look and experiencing yourself as "naughty."

Well it's time to get mother out of your bedroom. Your fears are centuries old emotionally. No one is going to blame or criticize you today if someone touches your wee-wee. You're a big girl now. Stop worrying about what nice girls do—or don't do. It's time to put aside those negative old tapes that say *any kind of touching or feeling good down there is bad.*

In the privacy of your adult life, it's okay for hands —yours or his—to touch you. All over, all over, all over. It's fine, good and healthy today.

When you see yourself tensing up or selling yourself a bill of goods that you're not in the mood, you might say, "Hey, are these my old tapes starting to play? Am I repeating my parents' negative views and fears about sex or my own? Am I playing my mother's tapes from ancient history, or am I going to allow myself to be a feeling, sensual woman right now?"

This is the moment when you can "stop the negative camera" and start thinking your own healthy, positive thoughts. *Stop all the negatives.* They aren't even your material. They are your parents' tapes. Whenever negative ideas do enter your mind when you're making love, you can *stop the camera* and start feeding a new, self-designed program into your emotional computer that comes from your adult ability to reason—your adult head. This tape can sound something like this:

"I'm with someone I care about. I want to relax and enjoy these feelings. Right now I'm going to try to get into this sweet pleasure. I want to think about how nice it feels *right now,* how cozy I am *right now* —how good it feels to be in the arms of someone I care about—*now.*

"For a few minutes at least I am going to postpone all the negative pictures that are running in my head. I'm going to stop the camera on what's wrong, what makes me angry or what I resent. I'm going to start the camera rolling with a new tape that says, 'What I'm doing now is good. I'm going to feel every minute of this. I'm going to relax, hang in, and just enjoy myself.' "

You have choice. You can take your negative ideas and quickly switch them to positive statements about your immediate environment (e.g., how cool the clean sheets are, how quiet and peaceful the room is) and yourselves (e.g., how good his body feels up close to you, how nice your skin feels, how comforting it is to be so close).

Once you've been able to soften the drone of your negative camera, you'll be ready for further exploration into your sensuality.

A New Dimension

In the PLEASURE PROCESS we're going to be exploring a kind of human interaction between two people that is far beyond what we normally refer to as sex—beyond orgasm and beyond sexual intercourse. Rather, it's a new kind of sensuality which blends the emotional wealth of a long lost erotic childhood history with one's contemporary potential for sensuality. All of this will meld into a new dimension, a new sexual experience for *you*.

Welcome to the PLEASURE PROCESS. You are about to be presented the key to your sensual power. Unlock it. Splendor in it.

Chapter 7

Step I:
Hugging

The evening has its arms about us now.

—LORD LLOYD FRANKENBERG

HUGGING is the first step in the PLEASURE PROCESS. Some of you may be saying, "Huh? Hugging doesn't sound very sensual to me." That's just the point. In this first step we're going to make a connection, a bridge back to early memories and experiences. I want you to recapture some of the sensual feelings you experienced when you were a baby being massaged, hugged and caressed; when you felt dependent and safe and cared for—without any pressure to perform or any anxieties about sex. The latter is especially important, because when you had your first erotic feelings, there were no concerns about sex. You were an infant, spontaneous and uninhibited.

This is why, now, in this first step, I want you to forget about sex for a while and let yourself enter into this special state of HUGGING. We're going to be moving into an *anti*-sex and *pro*-intimacy phase at first. Good sex, satisfying sex, rapturous sex, incredible sex, springs forth from *intimacy*.

In this first part of the PLEASURE PROCESS, cuddling is the main event. There will be *absolutely no attention to genitals or sex*. In fact, I want you to forget that you have genitals. All erogenous zones are to be put aside for now and genitals are to fade into the background.

A Transitory State

When you start thinking about having sex, I want you to take time out for an interim period: let yourself drift into a transitory state where you're *not* in the real world of talking, moving and sharing ideas from your normal day's activities, and you're not yet in the sexual world of erotic feelings and sensations.

There needs to be a winding-down phase, a transition that is neither sexual nor nonsexual. There needs to be a treading-water phase where you're suspended in time —resting, relaxing, feeling cared for and safe.

When you're moving from the real world of problem solving and planning into the sexual world, give yourself the time you will need to make this transition; it's very important for lovers to have this extra time.

In working toward gourmet sex via the PLEASURE PROCESS, I don't want you to think about your real world, or about sex. I don't want you to do *any* thinking. In this first step, HUGGING, I want you and your lover just to quietly hug each other, lying together in an almost motionless state, enjoying this simple activity: the sweet nothingness of hugging. Don't think about anything except the closeness, your skin and your body.

Very few people can get into the moment. What happens is that when they're eating they're thinking about something else like paying bills; when they're at work they're worried about what happened the night before;

and when they're playing tennis, they're thinking about how they didn't sleep well last night. Too often, people are out of sync, out of the moment. They're too far back into painful memories or too far forward into feared expectations to experience their *now*.

In the PLEASURE PROCESS, if you miss the moment, there's little chance to get in touch with the kind of sensitivity and sensuality you're going to need to enjoy yourself.

It's absolutely imperative in having good sex to stop the negative camera and forget about all the past or future negative tapes that you normally run through your head.

The Pleasure Process and Intimacy

For most people, intimacy can be a frightening and risky experience. While most of us can talk a good deal about wanting to be intimate, too often we become terrified when we are actually faced with it.

Real intimacy requires a willingness to be vulnerable, to share feelings, to be dependent, and to be truly honest. But being vulnerable means you're more open to getting hurt. So most people are afraid to chance it.

How to Become Intimate

Few people receive the kind of hugging and touching they need as children to set the initial steps of normal sexual development in motion. Most of us were raised by parents who themselves received too little physical caressing and affection and who consequently found being affectionately demonstrative strange and uncomfortable. Because we were deprived of these hugging experiences when we were children, it is unlikely that as adults we will have learned the necessary skills to be affectionate and tender during sex.

In the HUGGING step you will be able to fill in the affectional gaps that occurred in your childhood. It *is* possible to develop these skills as an adult, but in order to do this you have to recreate some of the original conditions that were present during your childhood.

During HUGGING, when the entire focus is on relaxing and capturing the warmth and intimacy of your body interlaced with your partner's, the emotional deficits that were created during your childhood can start to repair.

You may encounter some initial resistance from your partner in relation to this step because of his anxieties about hugging when he's not having sex. Many of my male patients complain when they are going through the PROCESS that they only feel comfortable hugging if they are actively engaged in either petting or intercourse.

When we discuss their early affectional interactions with their parents, these men explained that their parents rarely shared affection or even communicated in a warm and intimate manner, and that they, themselves, were rarely hugged. Affection for them was limited to a playful punch on the back or the arm, or a brief tousling of the hair. Parents are so concerned about turning their sons into sissies that most boys are denied the closeness and intimacy of affectionate embraces. Not until they are physically involved as adults in sexual activity is the cloak of the macho male allowed to drop off long enough for brief periods of hugging and intimacy to be tolerated. For most men, from infancy on, the experience of hugging is:

. . . almost all downhill. Not until we enter into the intimacy of sexual relations will we again fill the need for touching. And probably not even then. We don't turn off a basic need, keep it turned off for years, and expect it to respond the moment we press the "on" button. Inhibitions are not that easily overcome. And touching becomes one of our strongest inhibitions.[14]

Outside of sex the inhibitions against hugging will usually take over. Few men are able to say to their mates, "Honey, I'm too frightened to hug because I really don't know how. I never had any training." Rather, a man will say something like, "What's all this hugging nonsense? When do we get down to sex?" or "You have gained so much weight it's no fun to hug you." If these don't work, your partner may try to stop the HUGGING process by knocking on your hip with his erection and trying to distract you.

Any of the above will mean that it's too unfamiliar to him and he's too anxious to risk feeling intimate. This is a signal to you that you're going to need to stop for a while and try again later. Also, you're going to need to take a thoughtful look at yourself. If your mate can't tolerate much hugging—what about you? I believe that equal emotional partners find each other and fall in love. If he can't stand much hugging, my hunch is that your early encounters with hugging were limited, too. Talk more together about your childhoods, your experiences in touching, your feelings about your parents, affection, and so on. As you discuss your early histories, it will help you to better understand each other. Share in the struggle together while you move through the steps.

When a child grows up without having had role models to show him or her the way, this child can hardly be expected to understand how to practice being intimate as an adult. But you *both* can develop new skills now. You both can learn the language of intimacy. In the PLEASURE PROCESS, you and your partner will serve as the necessary role models for teaching affectionate intimacy to each other. You will dare to be vulnerable and honest and to present your unique and authentic selves.

Touching and Holding

Various studies have shown that physical contact is central to the normal emotional development of all mammals. This was demonstrated by H. F. Harlow in his studies on the nature of love and social deprivation in monkeys. Harlow discovered that if rhesus monkeys were separated from their mothers shortly after birth, their need for contact resulted in their clinging to surrogate mothers—even though these substitutes were nothing more than wire dummies covered with fabric.

Harlow also found that when infant monkeys were separated from both mother and peers, so that early bodily contact was absent or minimal, their affectional and sexual behaviors were seriously impaired.

Other than being fed, being held and touched is probably the most significant interaction underlying the development of a sense of security and comfort. This is true for all mammals, especially human infants.

Touching and holding are biologically based psychosocial patterns of behavior. The way people physically relate to other people largely depends on *how* they were touched during childhood, how *often* they were touched, and whether they were touched *at all*. As a result of this early body contact or lack of it, people establish certain patterns of relating as adults.

Some people are more comfortable in a passive role —being held and touched—and others in an active physical role—holding and touching. Other people are comfortable with almost no physical contact at all. As a therapist, it has been my observation that patients who have suffered high deprivation of physical affection in childhood are less able to tolerate physical closeness as adults. And often, they are prone to some form of sexual dysfunction. Indeed, one of the most important antecedent conditions in becoming a loving and sexually happy adult is to have experienced being touched as an infant through hugs, kisses, cuddles and caresses. Love and emotional security are absorbed as much "through the pores" as through "mother's milk."

Our need to be held and stroked, even as adults, cannot be overestimated. Often my male patients confide that they're having sex more frequently than they desire. What they really want is to be hugged and stroked, but they don't know how to ask for it and they're afraid that their need for affection isn't manly.

My female patients have similar concerns. They, too, express a longing for more affection and caressing in their lives. Women's need to be touched was demonstrated in a series of studies by Dr. Marc H. Hollender. In his research, Hollender discovered that some women want to be held more than they want genital sex. Rather they *used* sexual enticement to obtain their primary aim: *cuddling*. This study suggested that some women will go to extreme lengths to obtain this bodily contact, engaging in promiscuous behavior or even prostitution to gratify their need to be held.

No Sex for a While

In order to gratify your need to be held, in this initial step, HUGGING, there will be *no sex* for seven days. Does this sound difficult? Or are you relieved?

I want you to delay your sex and put it in a mental drawer for a while. Tuck it away, because the focus is going to be on intimacy—and only intimacy.

Your homework for this first step should be practiced seven times during seven different nights. Some of you may be able to practice your seven nights consecutively, Monday through Sunday, for example, and that will take a week. Others may take two weeks to cover their seven nights of practice.

Some of you will find that when you're into Step I of HUGGING you'll be so overtaken with passion and the joyous experience that you will find yourselves having sex before you realize it. Fine. Don't worry. You're not going to get a grade of "F" in HUGGING.

However, *that* evening won't be called a night of "doing the PLEASURE PROCESS." You can call that "just taking a night off and having a bit of fun."

When you are ready to get back to the PROCESS I want you to complete seven nights of just HUGGING before you go on to the next step. That is, make sure you have devoted a total of seven nights exclusively to this first step, even though you might have "slipped" once and had sex in between.

Repeat: *Practice Step I seven times before moving on to the next step.*

It's important to elicit the cooperation of your husband or sexual partner in this adventure. In fact, his wholehearted cooperation is vital.

Tell him that Dr. Kassorla guarantees incredible sex, in fact, gourmet sex, for you both if you can just slow down and indulge yourselves in seven nights of HUGGING *only*.

Too often couples get into bed feeling warm and affectionate toward each other, then too quickly move to a brief moment of foreplay and go immediately on to intercourse. Rarely is this enough to relax or stimulate a woman. As soon as the penis becomes erect, the race for orgasm begins. The woman feels angry and cheated. But in reality, in this kind of "quickie" sex, both partners are cheated. Intimacy ends and so does sensuality.

There are times when a "quickie" can be fun and rewarding for both partners. However, for many couples, four or five minutes of sex is all they ever experience. It's the entire fare.

One of the major reasons that sex rarely is sensual and passionate for most couples is because it starts too fast. One night one of my new patients laughingly noted that she and her husband normally spent exactly three minutes on foreplay. Well, that's barely enough time to adjust your bodies to the sheets and the mattress, let alone to call it foreplay.

For a while, I want you and your partner to forget about the concept of foreplay. We're moving into *a new concept of intimacy* and HUGGING, which needs to be instituted long before considerations of foreplay can be met.

A Time for Sweet Repose

Now take your partner's hand and find a place for sweet repose. Forget about time, and protect yourself from interruptions.

In this first phase you will learn how to remove yourself from the frustrations and restrictions of daily living with all its necessary rules and regulations. Break away from a structured order. Say goodbye to "shoulds" and "musts"; get ready now to practice your steps. Soon you will feel comfortable with the newness of the experience and find yourself loving it.

Step I: Hugging

In this first step, the concentration is on experiencing the pleasure of being held. It is in this state, in the safety of your lover's arms, that the emotional security essential to awakening and welcoming your erotic child is created.

Cast off your worries, along with your clothes. Lie down in your favorite hugging position and get comfortable. Nestle in.

Begin to cuddle.

Just hold each other quietly and closely *without* moving your arms or hands . . . skin to skin, intertwined. Avoid talking, as I want you to be totally aware of your body, your head, your arms, your torso, your legs.

Enjoy your awareness as you close your eyes
and *relax*.

Forget about everything except how wonderful your body feels. Cling to each other, feeling cozy and comfortable. Lull yourself into a tranquil state. Be a baby again, feeling cared for, adorable and safe. Take your time. Allow yourself at least 15 minutes on each of your nights for this step. You'll need at least 15 minutes to slowly unwind into a new, friendly environment—a stressless world without deadlines or responsibilities.

The focus is on *you*. In this first step I want to hammer home the importance of focusing on yourself.

Do not worry about your partner's feelings.
Do not watch your partner's face.
Do not monitor your partner's reactions.

That's his responsibility.

DON'T get involved in analyzing your partner's responses or you'll fall away from your own sexual feelings and become preoccupied in waiting for signs of his approval or disapproval.

The focus needs to be on you because in this initial stage the mind sends out special signals to the body, heralding the first subtle stirrings of sexual arousal. When you are able to concentrate totally on yourself, you'll be able to pick up these signals, and their intensity will increase.

Enjoy the nearness of the embrace . . .

How good it feels to have skin covering skin,
a warm sweet body close to your body.

As you ignore genitals and all erogenous areas, snuggle deeper into the hugging.

Remember, the focus is solely on you.
Enjoy your unique, original self.

I want you to say this to yourself: "I'm going to 'stop the negative camera' right now. I'm not going to think about what happened yesterday or what there is to worry about tomorrow. I'm going to stop all my negative tapes and I'm just going to do *this*."

And the "this" of the moment during sex is exactly what you're doing at that very second. Not what you did a minute before and not what you're going to do a minute later. I want you to stop your negatives and worries and just concentrate on what you're doing at *that very second*.

Concentrate on all the sensations, the feelings, the touching of skin where your body meets his. Concentrate on the smallest little thing that may be happening to you. Maybe a little tingle in your finger. *Concentrate on that*. Maybe a nice feeling in your back. *Concentrate on that*. Just hug your partner without any intention of going forward or going back. Just hug your partner and enjoy what's happening at that very moment.

No thinking.

No planning.

No expectations.

No worries.

Just lie there and hug . . . quietly . . . motionless . . . enjoying the moment.

Chapter 8

Step II:
Fingertipping

Be a god and hold me With a charm!
Be a man and fold me With thine arm!

—ROBERT BROWNING

Once you have practiced and enjoyed HUGGING for seven days, I want you to progress in the PLEASURE PROCESS to FINGERTIPPING. And this step will take another seven days.

Now, as we've said before, if you have sex on, say, the fourth night of either HUGGING or FINGERTIPPING, don't worry. While I'd prefer that you avoid it, in the event that it happens, it won't be called "night 4" of FINGERTIPPING. It will be a departure from the PROCESS, so you will still need a "night 4" to do your FINGERTIPPING. In order to derive the most complete benefit from these exercises, I want you and your partner to have seven nights of focusing in on HUGGING and then another seven nights of FINGERTIPPING.

The Largest Organ of Your Body

The skin is the largest organ of the human body, holding within its flexible form all other organs. Your skin is also your major source of sensory stimulation. You can live without your arms, legs, sight or hearing. And in this day of transplants you can survive with the surgical installation of many artificial organs. But if a large area of your skin is destroyed, you will die.

At birth, your mother welcomed you into the world by touching and caressing your baby skin. Contact was your first mode of human communication. Long before you learned to speak you communicated through touching, experiencing either the loving, protective, soft embrace of a parent, or the harsh, cruel touch of punishment or rejection.

Your skin is an overall agent for communication, as it both receives and delivers messages. From the moment of birth until the hour of death your skin is a telltale indicator of your reactions: you blush with embarrassment; perspire under stress; become livid with anger, pallid with fear, or aglow with sexual passion. Your skin will speak.

As a major sensory organ, your skin is perhaps the most important part of your body to come into play in the preparation for sensuality. Ashley Montagu explains that "the surface area of the skin has an enormous number of sensory receptors receiving stimuli of heat, cold, touch, pressure, and pain. . . . It is estimated that [the skin contains] some 50 receptors per 100 square millimeters, a total of 640,000 sensory receptors. Tactile points vary from 7 to 135 per square centimeter. The number of sensory fibers from the skin entering the spinal cord by the posterior roots is well over half a million!"[15]

Some people believe that it is necessary to stimulate only the skin of the erogenous zones in order to create pleasure. But the erogenous zones are *not* the only areas of the skin that can provide excitement. In FINGERTIPPING, the *entire* skin surface can become an erogenous zone.

This second phase has been designed to help you link up with the erotic sensations of childhood that were first experienced through your skin: being massaged and oiled after your bath; being cuddled in your mother's arms; being rocked and held close. This step will help you to recapture the sensuality that you enjoyed during infancy.

Step II: Fingertipping

After you have reestablished a sense of intimacy and security after seven nights of HUGGING, you are prepared to start the second step of the PROCESS, which I refer to as FINGERTIPPING.

In FINGERTIPPING, you will discover that the palm sides of your fingertips are among the most highly sensitized touch nerves in your body. As J. Lionel Taylor states in *The Stages of Human Life*, "The greatest sense in our body is our touch sense. It is probably the chief sense in the processes of sleeping and waking; it gives us our knowledge of depth or thickness and form; we feel, we love and hate, are touchy and are touched, through the touch corpuscles of our skin." Now, in the PROCESS, you will explore this sensitivity as you use a touch as delicate as that of a tiny spider:

> *The spider's touch, how exquisitely fine!*
> *Feels at each thread, and lives along the line.*
> —ALEXANDER POPE

The most convenient position for FINGERTIPPING will be lying on your sides. While continuing to hug, softly spill your fingers over your partner's back, as he does the same to you. Note that your backs will be the *only* areas you will be touching during this step.

Use very little pressure, as though you were fondling an infant.

Continue embracing as you proceed in a slow
and loving manner.

Fingertipping your partner's back lightly and rhythmically will have a relaxing and hypnotic effect. You will begin to reactivate and sensitize surfaces of skin that have been dormant since childhood. And the associations, feelings and sensual images that have been dormant since then will begin to be reactivated as well.

The easy, rhythmical motions of being fingertipped will signal associations to resurface that you originally enjoyed during the rocking and fondling rituals of infancy. These images will start trickling out into awareness as you draw your fingertips over each other's backs. Concentrate on the wonderful sensations you are receiving. While you fingertip your partner, remember to keep the focus on you. Begin to learn how to concentrate fully on yourself as you *listen to your skin.*

"It should be noted that sex is not a basic need since the survival of the organism is not dependent upon its satisfaction. Only a certain number of organisms need satisfy sexual tensions if the species is to survive. However that may be, the evidence points unequivocally to the fact that *no organism can survive very long without externally originating cutaneous stimulation,*" according to Ashley Montagu in *Touching.* [Italics added.]

And in terms of psychological importance, the closeness and physical warmth of a caring other, and the laying on of caressing hands are essential to *emotional survival.*

In FINGERTIPPING, although the two of you are joined together physically, you are still thinking and feeling separately . . . and there is so much to feel. At first your center of attention will be on your back and the tingling sensations in your fingertips. Before long, you'll be surprised to find that you are experiencing sensations in parts of your body that *aren't even being touched.*

Every part of you is coming awake and responding.

Your skin becomes the core of your world.

Patients working on the PROCESS often ask why conventional massage won't work just as well. The typical massage will not get the results we're looking for here. The reason is that in most massage rituals one person is the *doer* and the other is the receiver, a performance procedure that is unequal in terms of giving and receiving. In these first steps of the PLEASURE PROCESS, performance has been carefully eliminated so that partners may share equally in the experience. Each person behaves the same way, stroking the other's back. The task is so simple and so repetitive that performance anxieties abate.

You will experience peacefulness in the simplicity of FINGERTIPPING. You won't need to be anxious, wondering about what to expect next. It will always be the same: a slow, feathery, almost monotonous tracing on each other's back.

One of my patients explained:

I'm so used to performing and doing something significant during sex that I was surprised to see that just relaxing and gently fingertipping each other's back would be so hard to do. At first it was really tough for me to cycle down and do something so simple. But after about the fourth day of trying this step, we were both able to relax and get into it. Just to lie there quietly holding and feeling the steady sensations on my back got my entire skin into a trickling and trembling trance.

These first two steps start the initial tapping into the subconscious to recapture the erotic child within you. You are being nurtured physically by the fingertipping and emotionally by tender feelings that are reminiscent of the warmth and trust you knew as an infant.

As Montagu continues in *Touching:*

The manner in which the young of all mammals snuggle up to and cuddle the body of the mother as well as the bodies of their siblings or of any other introduced animal strongly suggests that cutaneous stimulation is an important biological *need,* for both their physical and behavioral development. Almost every animal enjoys being stroked or otherwise having its skin pleasurably stimulated. Dogs appear to be insatiable in their appetite for stroking, cats will relish it and purr, as will innumerable other animals both domestic and wild.

By the time you reach this second step you'll start to understand how the peaceful intimacy of HUGGING and FINGERTIPPING will generate a whirlpool of sensations that will eventually extend throughout your body. All your skin will come alive as your own sensual electricity is created.

To let this process unfold:

Do not touch genitals . . . yet.

Do not touch *any* erogenous zones . . . yet.

Limit yourselves exclusively to the area of each other's backs during this exercise. This is *not* the step in which you will be sexually inventive and explorative, because in Steps I and II:

ALL EROGENOUS ZONES ARE OFF LIMITS!

If you do start stimulating genitals in these first two steps, it will inhibit the possibility of the *entire* surface of your skin becoming an erogenous zone. But if you give yourself time, and practice the PLEASURE PROCESS steps as I described them, eventually you may achieve orgasm just by being hugged or by having your back, a foot, or an arm touched. In order for this to happen, you must remember to:

Focus on you.

Listen to your skin.

Enjoy the full excitement of the sensations.

Limit the gentle, easy fingertipping to each other's backs . . . and zero into

enjoying your unique, original self.

It Takes Time

In this step, your focus has continued to remain on *you*. Your total involvement has been directed toward concentrating on the sensations of your skin. By ignoring genitals, and by focusing on only a small portion of the body (in this case, the back), the mind isn't distracted. The repetitive stroking is so simple that you won't be thinking about positions, planning or performance. Total attention can be paid to receiving sensations and listening to your skin.

As in HUGGING, it is important to proceed slowly in order to establish an atmosphere of intimacy, security and safety. You move slowly in FINGERTIPPING for still another reason—it takes time for the skin to awaken sensually and build to an erotic level.

By moving in this slow-motion cadence and by delaying the sexual satisfaction of petting and intercourse, you'll be fostering a climate in which neither partner will feel used or exploited, where you'll both know what it means to be cared for and wanted—not as sexual objects, but as people.

The slow, stroking movements of FINGERTIPPING can lead you into a hypnotic state where the mysteries of your sensual "past" will unite with your adult "present" to create a dramatically new sensuality, utilizing all the hidden potential of your mind and body.

There is a good deal of repetition in these first two steps. I do this deliberately because there is so much blocking and fear linked up with sexuality and intercourse that, before we can actually relax and feel safe enough to deal with our FORBIDDEN tapes and dare to be sensual, these old fears must be quieted.

The slow pace of the first two steps will allow you to sort through some of your old emotional garbage and risk feeling intimate without the anxieties of thinking and performing during sex, protected in the safe harbor of your lover's arms.

Chapter 9

Step III:
Silence Isn't Golden

And when Love speaks, the voice of all the gods
Makes heaven drowsy with the harmony.

—SHAKESPEARE

Once you've learned to be comfortable and more familiar with your HUGGING and FINGERTIPPING homework, I want you to add a new dimension to them . . . the freedom of talking to each other during your sex. Throughout the various steps of the PLEASURE PROCESS, new techniques of learning are integrated. One of the most important to consider is how to express yourself verbally when you're sexual—how to unlock your tongue and learn your own original language of sensuality.

In our normal lives speech serves many purposes. With the people with whom we are the closest, speech often is used as a smoke screen to hide important feelings. We use sarcasm to hide anger; we criticize to hide feelings of inadequacy; and we scream and holler as a cover-up when we are really hurting.

Some people use speech to manipulate; others use silence as a way to punish or stay in control. Some of us talk constantly when we're feeling anxious and uncomfortable. We use speech to reduce anxiety, chattering endlessly and meaninglessly whenever we feel frightened.

Ideally, in an interpersonal relationship, speech can be used to accurately communicate ideas to your mate, offer information, explain needs and wants, discuss motivations and aspirations and share feelings. Unfortunately, this idea is rarely actualized. As a consequence, many psychological and emotional problems result. We feel frustrated by our inability to express our real feelings to the people we love. This is especially true in the area of sex.

When we were children, few of us had the opportunity to talk about sex with our parents. It simply wasn't allowed as a subject for discussion in most families. We were led to believe that talking (and even thinking) about sex was almost as bad as "doing it." If we dared to ask curious questions, the answers we received were, typically, hesitating and awkward. Our parents gave us terse replies, sudden changes in the subject, the silent treatment, and in the extreme, severe punishment. It was okay to talk about toys or friends or problems, but not sex.

As we grew older, the more intellectual our conversation, the better: it was fine to extol the ecstasies of a gorgeous sunset, a sleek car, a delicious banquet, or a Monet tree dripping into a lake. We could talk about anything—anything, that is, except *sex*.

Finally, we become adults. But, alas, nothing changes! We're still not supposed to talk about sex, and particularly not while we're having it. Consequently, during sexual play and intercourse, most of us are mute! Our early training has resulted in an inbred silence. This makes it almost impossible for most of us to discuss our needs and preferences in bed. Our early conditioning has taken its toll.

Many women are dead in bed—almost corpselike—because society and parents have trained them to believe that this is the way *nice girls* should be: nonaggressive and *silent*.

"No noise, girls. Any aggressive behavior will be considered trashy and vulgar. So settle down. Just lie there like quiet clunks: no movements, no talk, and no orgasms."

Lowering the Floodgates

When you can lower the floodgates on speaking and allow talk to enter the bedroom, a wealth of old associations will have the opportunity to emerge.

> *Releasing the brake on the tongue results*
> *in releasing the brake on the subconscious.*

We need the freedom to talk in the bedroom that we have at the table. We have license to be sensual when we look at food. In the motion picture *Tom Jones* the world understood and accepted that the sensual "ohs" and "ahs" in relation to food were appropriate. Society *allows* us to look at food and to moan and groan.

We can examine a banquet table and become ecstatic with "Oh, my, isn't this beautiful! Just smell these gorgeous delicacies! Don't they look wonderful? I can't wait to get them in my mouth." This is fine; this is acceptable behavior.

We can look at a baby and be sensual in our comments: "Did you ever see anything so precious, so soft, so sweet? Oh, I love the way he feels! I love to touch his skin! What a round, firm little body!" This kind of sensuality is acceptable.

We are also allowed to be sensual when commenting on nature. Looking at the ocean, we can say we are thrilled with the sounds, the magnificence, the overwhelming, enveloping wetness. We can also be passionate in examining inanimate objects such as art or flowers or a landscape or the serenity of a pastoral scene.

But sex? No talking during sex! Ssh, sssh, ssh! We've got to be quiet. We mustn't say a word. And so we miss out on another important element that could help us in freeing our sensuality and increasing our sexual pleasure.

Stop the "sshing" and trust yourself.

Share your sensations during sex.

Share your thoughts, the pictures in your head.
Talk, talk, talk!!

As you learn to free up your tongue and you do start talking about what you're feeling, you'll begin to notice that unconscious images—long-buried objects, faces, and events from your childhood—will come onto the TV screen in your mind. In whatever disguises these images appear, whether sensual or nonsensual, *talk about them*.

We discussed how the erotic child buries everything away in a beautiful hidden room. Well now it's time for these treasures to start emerging. At first, some of this erotica appears in substitute forms—images that seem totally unrelated to sex. But since they are emerging at precisely the time when you *are* making love, *there is a connection*. Respect this connection. Trust its importance and share it with your mate.

Gradually, as you practice your talking, the images will leave your subconscious and slip into your awareness. This talking will act as a summons, an invitation welcoming your erotic child to enter your sexual life again. You and your partner will find that this kind of sharing brings forth a flood of sensuality, deepening your mutual feelings of love and intimacy.

Releasing the Brakes

In order for women to release the brakes on their vaginas, they need first to release their verbal and physical brakes. I encourage women who are strangers to their sensuality to get acquainted with the notion that talking during sex is healthy and normal.

Listen in on a conversation I had with a patient who was struggling with this problem.

SILENT SHARON

When Sharon, a nonorgasmic patient, first came in for therapy, she told me that her husband would *never* accept talking during sex.

"Regardless of what comes into your head," I nonetheless urged, "say it. Try it on. It's fun."

"Are you kidding?" Sharon argued. "If ever I'd say a word to my husband, he would probably lose his erection and blame me. Then I'd never hear the end of it."

"You can both learn to have the freedom to talk during sex," I explained. "It's normal and healthy to share feelings and sensations. Talk about your bodies and what you're seeing in your minds. It's fun to talk during sex—about anything. You can be silly and nonsensical and playful. Share the excitement. Don't analyze what you're saying or try to make sense out of it—just erupt, talk!"

"But I don't want to lose control," explained Sharon. "It makes me feel crazy. When I talk, my body seems to start talking, too!"

"That sounds great to me," I said enthusiastically. "It would be good for you to give up control, Sharon. Your sensuality doesn't have a chance to flourish when you're holding back. Your sensuality will let go when *you* let go."

"That worries me." The patient sounded frightened. "When I keep talking and moving I start feeling too nervous. I'm afraid I'll have an epileptic seizure or something terrible will happen to me, like spinning off into space. I'm afraid."

"I *do* want you to lose control," I insisted. "In good sex, control goes out the window. The normal controls we use in everyday language and behavior need to be thrown away. In order to experience yourself fully during sex I want you to let your mind, body and words travel freely, without worrying or braking. Let it all out. Let yourself happen, verbally and physically. With a loving, caring partner, losing control is fine. In fact, you'll see that it will be *wonderful!*"

After a few months of therapy this patient learned how to share what was happening to her body and how to feel more sensual during lovemaking. She explained her newly discovered sensuality this way:

I just know I'm safe. I trust myself now, and I trust my husband, too. I used to think all the time during sex. I was always worried about my husband's feelings or whether he was close to coming. Now I just forget everything. I concentrate on his body and voice and my body and my sounds. I close my eyes and seem to fall away. It's almost like being in a hypnotic state—a sweet, slow-motion trance where all I want to do is listen to our voices and listen to my skin.

Your talking will excite your partner and the reverse will be true as well. When you can get your lover talking, as Sharon did just by verbalizing her own feelings, here's what can happen. Sharon continues:

One night when my husband was kissing me, I couldn't believe what came out of his mouth. It was "roller skates." Imagine! That isn't sexy! But he sounded so happy. He said the roller skates were sliding in a slippery, soft way all over my body, kissing me.

It didn't make sense to me, but I thought what he said was funny, and childlike. It made me feel good. Can you believe it? I started getting into the idea of those roller skates gliding softly over my body. I actually saw and felt them! I loved all those sliding wheels gently kissing me.

Then, my husband said the roller skates were bouncing along the street. They roamed into the motorcycle repair factory. I thought it was so silly —you know, cycles and skates. I kept listening to his voice, laughing. I repeated over and over, "I feel so hot, honey, so hot."

I told him how sweet his hands were, playing with me. Then both of us began using street jive like Hell's Angels. We kept making love and talking as the skates and cycles continued rolling around the hallways of the motorcycle repair factory.

I got so hot, I started coming as he sucked my breasts. And he wasn't even touching my vagina!

Helping this patient to give up control and unlock her verbal behavior during intercourse was an important part of the therapy. Encouraging her to openly share her fantasies and images regardless of the sensibleness of their content—without thinking and judging herself negatively—led her into a multi-orgasmic state.

You and your partner can work *together* on your sexual hang-ups and anxieties. Talk about your sexual fears and conflicts openly and honestly. Learn to appreciate and accept the innocence and excitement of talking and sharing images and fantasies during sex. Develop your own fresh and unique brand of friendly, fun sex talk.

Sometimes this kind of sharing is in the style of a Bachian concert. One partner starts on a particular theme, while the other may be speaking about a totally unrelated image. Both partners are accepting of each other's fantasy while playing happily and joyfully with their own.

At other times during sex one partner will start fantasizing about a particular image and the other may join in. This is their special fantasy time together. They can weave and interplay their images together in conjoint harmonies.

I've had similar results with other patients. While having intercourse, they've learned to accept and release the words in their heads without censure, enjoying themselves or their partners. They just flow. And as the words flow, so do the juices, the orgasms and the fun. Each partner sharing with his or her mate while capturing the physical ecstasy of their sex, together, in this loving experience.

In this step you'll come to understand why "silence isn't golden." Learning to talk during sex will serve many positive functions, because releasing the brake on your tongue will have an important psychological effect that will also result in releasing the brake on your body and your inhibitions. And most important, it will help to release much of your old repressed material. You will learn that verbalizing can be an erotic tool.

Ovid said that "love must be fostered with soft words." By verbalizing, you will both feel freer to love and to let go. Neither of you will need to worry about what's happening with your partner. Instead of trying to interpret vague groans and gyrations, you'll have specific and immediate feedback. This positive feedback is important. It will free you from the anxieties that approval seeking causes. Talking will allay these anxieties. Anxieties detract from the magic. They interfere with your awareness of yourself.

One of the basic ingredients of healthy sex talk is that it is *positive*. Criticism, negatives and complaints will destroy the mood of your precious sexual moments.

The following exercise is to be practiced when you're alone. It is designed to help you learn how to be more positive as you begin to talk during sex. As you become more skilled, you can practice this same exercise in bed.

EXERCISE 9: LEARNING TO USE POSITIVE SEX TALK

In this step it is important to share the good feelings you are experiencing. Don't just think them to yourself.

Say them out loud!

It will heighten the level of arousal for both of you. When you are secure in the knowledge that your partner is communicating what he is feeling, you will be relieved of the job of monitoring. Then, you're released to concentrate on your own feelings.

There are no limits as to style or variety of your positive sex talk. You can use anything from a foreign accent to a Southern drawl. Whether it's bawdy slang, sophisticated dialogue, baby talk, poetry or pornography, street or parlor language, everything you say about you that is positive and keeps the mood happy and sensual is *fine*.

Here are some examples of positive sex talk that you can use to start. The phrases I've listed below will give you a guideline about what you can say.

Repeat them out loud.

As you become more comfortable, the words will make an unconscious transfer, and you'll find yourself verbalizing while making love. You'll be creating more of your own phrases and erotic talk, and using less of mine. As you continue to do this, you will be encouraged to focus on each of your body sensations as they occur.

Whether you begin with my suggestions, or phrases of your own, isn't important.

What *is* important is that you talk about *you*.

Be positive and remember that *silence isn't golden* in bed.

Go to your mirror now with your book in hand. Look into the mirror and talk to you: Start saying this list of healthy, positive comments out loud. Even though it may seem strange to be making these statements when you're alone and not a bit aroused, let yourself say them anyway. I want you to become familiar with their sound. Then they'll no longer frighten you, and you'll be able to use them in the appropriate setting when you *are* feeling sensual.

Repeat them out loud, to *you*, several times:

—"I feel so good."
—"I love the tingling sensations on my body."
—"My skin seems silky and smooth."

—"I am so relaxed."

—"I feel so soft."

—"I'm so excited."

—"I have a warm throbbing in my vagina."

—"I'm a sensual woman."

—"I feel great and so sexy."

—"I'm so wet between my legs."

—"I can feel the tingling in my feet."

—"My nipples feel so hard."

—"My vagina is swelling."

—"I love my body."

—"I'm so happy."

—"I feel wonderful all over."

It's important to let these words roll off your tongue and have your ears hear them.

I want you to practice this exercise as often as you can, because learning to verbalize will be a first step in breaking down inhibitions. If at first you think you sound awkward and foolish, don't worry.

New behaviors develop slowly.

With practice, being aware of all your sensations and feelings will get easier, and so will talking positively about yourself. Your new speech habits will help you to erase old taboos, which will allow you to be more verbal and spontaneous in bed.

Altering the Conditions

For those of you who are comfortable masturbating, alter the conditions of this exercise. Say the list out loud to yourself while masturbating when you're alone. You can repeat one phrase over and over, or use several of the ones I've listed. Say whatever comes into your head that is positive about the sensuality you are feeling. Try on a smile and giggle a bit, too, as you talk. Enjoy yourself.

EXERCISE 10: TALKING AND AWARENESS

I want you to lie down during this exercise, alone, in a quiet, comfortable place where you won't be disturbed. Close your eyes. You will remember that in an earlier exercise you learned how to address every limb and muscle as you silently told yourself to relax.*

Building on that exercise, you will now introduce speech. You will be aware of your body and talk out loud about every sensual part. As in the relaxing exercise, start with your head and move down slowly, thinking about each part as you talk about it out loud.

This exercise consists of two sequences.

PART ONE

Begin first by saying:

"Now I am aware . . . aware of the skin on my face . . . how good it feels when I'm being stroked . . . how soft and sensitive it is to be touched."

Visualize each part of your body as you speak.

Enjoy each part of your body as you *speak*.

Remember how unique, original and wonderful you are.

Get used to the sound of your voice being sensual.

---

* Chapter 2, Exercise 1

"Now, I am aware of my mouth. I am opening it as I speak aloud my awareness . . . I feel so good . . . so alive . . . I love having my lips kissed.

"I am aware of my jawline . . . I can feel the firm bones.

"I am aware of my cheeks . . . I can feel them moving as I speak . . . I enjoy having my cheeks fondled."

Go down the length of your body, and discuss your awareness, as you visualize each part.

PART TWO

Once you are finished, repeat the exercise. This time, I would like you to add your sense of touch. That is, in addition to talking, *touch yourself* as you go, tracing your fingers over your skin.

Get acquainted with the "ups" and "downs," the "ins" and "outs" of your body.

Experience every sensation . . . be aware . . .
verbalize every sensation.

EXERCISE 11: LOOSENING UP VERBALLY

In your early social training you learned many "dos" and "don'ts" governing the use of certain words. But these very words that shocked your parents when you were small can be exciting in the bedroom now that you're big.

I want you to be able to expand your repertoire of language during sex to include some of those old "dirty" words that were "no-nos" when you were a child. You will find that allowing yourself this erotic freedom with your speech will be contagious. It will spread to other erotic areas and heighten your general level of sensuality.

Using these words may be very strange and uncomfortable for many of you. So start to do this at first when you're alone. Begin by whispering aloud to yourself every four-letter word you can think of.

Try not to leave anything out.

It will help you to write down the words as you go. Both speaking them out and writing them down will serve to reduce your toxic reaction to them.

Read your list over and repeat each word several times in your normal voice. When you are finished, go back over your list. But this time, try shouting the words out. Screaming them aloud to yourself will seem strange at first—but so much fun, you'll probably end up laughing. However, I caution you to close all windows so your neighbors won't go into shock!

Silence Isn't So Golden

Too many negative emotions are associated with silence. When people are angry, they are silent. When they are hurt, they are silent. When they feel inadequate or embarrassed, they are silent.

I want you to erase all the negative connections you have about silence. Take all the positive feelings you have already established about feeling good and talking and transfer them to sex. Remember that silence isn't so golden during sex.

When people are happy in situations outside of sex, they can be jubilant, talkative and share their pleasure. This is considered to be acceptable, normal behavior. It's important for you to learn to express yourself in this same manner during sex. But don't limit your loving words to the bedroom, because good sex starts long before you reach the bedroom.

Part of every day needs to be filled with loving words and gentle caresses. Whether or not you're planning to have sex, feeling warm and accepted breeds the sort of atmosphere in which sexual feelings can develop. It's difficult to feel close and affectionate after a day of harassment, so develop and nurture a tender mood. Only foolish lovers wait until they hit the sheets before they deliver positive words and feelings.

If you're together all day, be sure to start your affectionate hugging and touching as soon as you can. If you're away at work, try to telephone with warm messages like:

—"I feel so good when I'm with you."
—"I began missing you soon after I drove away."
—"I've been thinking about how good you smell."
—"I can't wait to see your smile."

When you establish an affectionate and positive atmosphere hours before you begin having sex, a happy mood is set. Words are powerful mood setters. You or your partner may be feeling anxious and inadequate even thinking about having sex, so it's important to create a safe and secure harbor.

Loving words can help to do this. And once your lovemaking has begun, your words will embellish your sexual feelings. Let yourself experience the erotic use of words. Let your partner in on all the sensations you're feeling; everything that's happening to your body and how excited you are. When you hear your partner saying, "I'm having such a good time!" it will be easier for you to relax and concentrate on your own good feelings.

Silence during lovemaking breeds alienation, increases anxiety, and squelches performance.

Talking promotes self-confidence, stimulates action, and encourages intimacy.

Enjoy your precious sexual moments as you begin unlocking your tongue.

Learn the language of real intimacy and sensuality.

Learn the language of love.

Chapter 10

Step IV:
Letting the Images Flow

Lovers remember all things.
—OVID

You're now ready for another joyful aspect of the PLEASURE PROCESS—the sharing of the erotic images that you will be discovering in your beautiful hidden room. At first, you may be afraid to talk about them because they'll seem to be unrelated to what's happening to you in bed. But it's worth taking the risk if you can repeat to your partner anything that flashes into your head. When you do, you'll be surprised to see how your vagina will explode. Let's look now at what happened to this patient.

JANET TAKES A CHANCE

As we discussed earlier, erotic images often appear in nonthreatening, nonsensual disguises. Here's an example that Janet, a 31-year-old patient who owns a small candy store, shared in my Monday night group therapy session.

I really took a chance last night. For weeks now my husband and I have been talking about the things we all discuss in group here. I've been explaining to him how important it is to talk about your erotic feelings during sex, but I've always been afraid to actually do it. I thought he'd start laughing at me if I did.

Well, last night when he was playing with my thighs, I suddenly flashed on the pediatrician I had when I was a little girl. I remembered he was a sweet, fat old man who was bald-headed. His name was Dr. Rosenbloom. I used to love him because he was so gentle—and he gave me suckers every time I went in for an examination.

When I first saw his face I thought I'd better not say anything because it would turn my husband off. Then I remembered the things we've shared in the group and I thought, what the heck, I'll give it a try. I started talking about Dr. Rosenbloom as my husband was kissing my thighs. When the old doctor used to touch my legs, it must have turned me on even though I was just a child. So talking about him examining me, while my husband was kissing my legs, set off an explosion of orgasms. In fact they came so fast while I was talking about that old man that it was almost involuntary—they just kept happening.

Not only didn't my husband criticize me, he got the hardest erection I've ever felt! We really had fun. So my advice to all of you is: take a chance. This talking stuff really works!

The first time you risk sharing with your mate an early flash or bit of information that comes into your head, you, too, will discover that these old bits and pieces are like atom bombs of sensuality—catalysts that will lead you into your avalanche of orgasmic responses.

Children are far more sexual than people realize. The child from birth to six is experiencing erotica, but not as adults understand it. It is *not* necessarily a sexual erotica, but it *is* erotica—erotica of form and movement and touch. As children we don't necessarily relate this to genitals, because we do not yet understand the relationship of genitals to sex. Nonetheless, we are able instinctively to experience this erotica.

As an adult, it is possible for you to tap into all of this erotica. To start with, you need to accept and talk about all of your nonerotic images. When you do, you will discover that as your images emerge and their disguises melt away, new dimensions of your sexuality will be revealed. You'll be surprised to find that these dimensions will be exciting to your partner, too—as well as to yourself: You'll *both* be delighted with the results.

Here is the most important message I have to give you, and I will repeat it over and over again:

To unleash your sensuality and use it today, first you must unbrake—unrepress—uninhibit your childhood erotica—you must go back and do an unlocking process.

Sexuality does not begin in adulthood. After approximately two decades of constant repression (through your early formative years and up to your twenties), you have learned that "Thou shalt not touch thyself," as well as "You mustn't let the boys touch you," "You mustn't look or feel down there," and "Nice girls don't." And after all this has been hammered and hammered and mashed and mashed and pounded in—using the analogy of the women in the Mediterranean who take the wash to the river and pound away and pound away

at the dirt until the dirt is released from the fabric—
you might assume that, in fact, your sensuality is all
washed away. But it *isn't* all washed down the river. As
I said before, it goes into your hidden room, where it
waits to be rediscovered.

The years roll by, and you become an adult. You get
married, and suddenly all signals are "go." Even your
parents nod their heads with a big smile and say, "Okay,
darling, it's time to be sexy." But you know what? It
isn't easy to be sexy after so much hammering and
mashing and pounding away at your sensuality. And
you can guess what's finally left of it after all those
years—just guilt.

Guilt acts like a traffic jam. Imagine a busy intersec-
tion in your hometown. Cars are piled up for blocks,
bumper to bumper going each way. Nothing can happen. Everything stands still. Nothing can get through.
Well, this is what guilt is like. Guilt acts like a traffic
jam in your mind that eventually spills over into your
body, blocking the flow of feelings so that no sensuality
can get through. Nothing can pass. There's no place
to go; there's no room. All the natural beauty of the
sensuality you came endowed with as a child is sub-
merged and replaced by guilt. So by the time you're
an adult, there's no sign of it left. All that remains is
a "nice girl"—you—a walking mass of sexual guilt.

Beginning the Unlocking Process

Before we start Step IV it is important that your partner
have as much information as you do about the PLEA-
SURE PROCESS and a clear understanding of how getting
in touch with your erotic child and reentering your
hidden room will enhance your sensuality and your intimate experiences together.

Before You Reach the Bedroom

When you're alone together during one of those comfortable moments, long before you're in the bedroom, share the philosophy of the PLEASURE PROCESS with your partner. Explain that what you're trying to do is get in touch with your early memories. When you can unlock these memories and share them with him, you'll find it akin to putting the key into the magic door of your sensuality.

You set the example. You start sharing little bits of your FORBIDDEN past. When you do, you'll see that his reactions will be so positive, your fears and doubts will vanish, and you'll be encouraged to go on and share more. And before long he'll be using you as a model, remembering and sharing his own precious secrets from childhood.

When you can both do this, when you can first share your images in a nonthreatening, nonsexual environment, it will be easier for you to come up with these images when they pop into your head and share them with each other when you're in bed.

Here's a way to start. Here are some examples of what you can say:

Honey, today, I'm not sure why, but I started thinking about the way I used to peek through the keyhole and watch my older brother take a bath. I used to love the excitement of sneaking and waiting. I would stay glued to that keyhole, praying for a glimpse of his penis. I started doing this when I was only three.

Dr. Kassorla explained to me that because I am so worried about your misunderstanding my sexy feelings from childhood, I hide them from you.

This could interfere with my really enjoying you and our love and sex right now.

I want you to know that I'm so turned on by you . . . so excited by you . . . that our sex sometimes stirs up a memory from childhood.

Instead of my keeping this so secretive and using so much emotional energy to hide it, I want to bring it all out into the open. I want to tell myself and you that it was okay to peek and watch through that keyhole . . . and that I can stop feeling so guilty. I want to spend my fun and energy in the present and enjoy myself more now with you

Dr. Kassorla said if I can feel free to talk about my childhood erotic images while we're making love, and you can accept and understand me without judging or criticizing me, it will add to the passion in our love life.

It's better to get it all out when it comes into my mind, because if I keep holding everything down inside of me, I can't give all of my emotional energy to our lovemaking. I'm too swamped and guilty with my past.

So tonight I want to just let it go. Whatever comes —I want to let it happen. If I start talking about anything that sounds off the wall, it's because I'm unblocking and opening up totally so I can be completely turned on with you.

After delivering this kind of message to your partner and making love a few times, it will become easier to share. It won't be so frightening.

Before long *his* mind will be tumbling back and he, too, will be unlocking and unblocking his childhood memories—such as the first time he had an erection, the first time he had a nocturnal emission, the day he saw his sister nude, and the night he slept with the cousin he was in love with, the time he played doctor with the little girl next door. You will both begin talking about your early erotica and sharing your images in tandem during sex.

Don't censor yourself.

Let it all flow.

The Playground for Your Erotic Past

Once you rid yourself of your inhibitions about talking during sex, a flood of old associations will surface.

As you become more skilled with the PROCESS, your bedroom will become a playground for your erotic past. You'll envision many different kinds of images during your lovemaking. Some will be direct projections of old memories. Others will be fantasies based on your sexual history.

Here is a case history that will help you to understand how some of my patients have unearthed their hidden erotica.

DOUG'S DISCOVERY

Last year I treated Doug and Louise both in private therapy and in group. Doug is lean, fortyish and handsome, with a lion's mane of thick golden-brown hair. He is a regional distributor for foreign car replacement parts.

Louise, who is five years younger than Doug, is constantly fighting a weight problem, hiding her body under flowing caftans. She works part-time as a nursery-school teacher and spends the rest of her time as a homemaker raising their two teenage daughters.

The family lives on an oak-lined street in a pretty, middle-class suburb just north of Los Angeles.

When Doug and Louise first married their sex was frequent and exciting. They both experienced a great deal of pleasure and sexual fulfillment. But after the first two years, the excitement waned and Doug started sleeping with other women.

When Louise found out about Doug's extramarital carryings-on, she was really hurt. Their sex life came to a virtual standstill and Louise started talking about divorce.

Doug persuaded Louise to enter therapy, and together they came in to see me.

After many months of working on their problems and learning how to communicate better, Doug stopped his philandering. Slowly, their sex life resumed. However, sex was still uninteresting for both of them.

It was at this point that we started working on the PLEASURE PROCESS, beginning with HUGGING and FINGERTIPPING. Soon after, they started to verbalize a little during their sex.

One night during intercourse, as Doug held Louise's ample buttocks in his hands, he saw an image. He began to talk out loud as their lovemaking continued:

I see a crack in the door.

Louise encouraged him:

Look through the crack, Doug, and tell me what you see.

Doug hesitated:

I'm afraid to look in . . . it's too scary. If my mommy catches me she'll spank me.

Louise answered:

Keep talking, honey. What can you see?

Feeling reassured, Doug continued:

I think it's the bathroom in the old house. I can see our neighbor through the crack in the door. She's undressing. She comes here every Saturday morning to weigh herself. She's always dieting and she's so fat. She leaves the door ajar, and I always sneak up to watch her. It makes my penis feel so hard and good.

Louise said:

You're making me so hot, I love this!

Doug was laughing now:

Honey! Can you believe it? I've never felt this hard. I feel so powerful.

Louise was orgasming when she said:

Keep talking, honey. You've got me so crazy, I can't stop coming. I see something too. It's a little girl looking through a keyhole. It's me! I'm watching something. Oh! I can see my grandfather's balls. He just got out of the tub. They are so big and so long . . . my whole body feels hot.

Doug kept talking about his image, almost as though he hadn't heard Louise:

Can you believe what a fat ass my mom's friend has! I'd love to bury my face in it. Oh, I feel so good . . . I'm so hard.

Doug and Louise continued making love throughout the night, alternately sleeping, cuddling, talking, and having intercourse. They had never felt closer.

During their next therapy session with me, Louise, looking very thoughtful, said laughingly to Doug:

No wonder you keep bringing home pastries and candy! You really don't want me to lose weight, do you?

Doug leaned over and kissed her affectionately,

You bet your sweet fat ass I don't! You're perfect . . . just the way you are.

When we learn that Doug's curiosity as a young boy led him to peek at his mother's friend as she undressed, or that Louise sneaked a look at her nude grandfather, we know this is harmless and we instantly forgive them —and *they* forgive *themselves*. We find such childhood escapades so innocent that we discount their significance when we flash back to them as adults. It is hard to believe that they could be so important as to influence our sex lives today.

When we bury our childhood erotica into our subconscious, we don't have the wealth of experience in life and sensuality that we do as adults. We don't realize the magnitude of what we're doing. We are reacting to having been reprimanded or thwarted in some way by our parents. We assume that what we've done is reprehensible. We never want to even think of it again because it reminds us of the disapproval we felt then. Disapproval from a loving parent is so painful that the child needs to block out any remnants of these feelings.

The advantage of being able to unearth this erotica now is that we can both release something that is healthy and erase an early experience in life that we once labeled as "wicked" and "unpardonable." As adults we feel inadequate because of all the guilty moments that we have stuffed into our unconscious. Taking an adult look at these "FORBIDDEN sins" allows us to appreciate how normal they all were.

The more of this you can do—that it, taking a second look at your childhood guilts—the more adequate you will feel as an adult. These realizations will affect your whole life more positively: at work, with your family, and with your friends and community.

RECURRING IMAGES

Sometimes you and your partner will be talking about something that is similar and saying things almost simultaneously. Let them blend together, each one's image playing its chorus against the other's in concert. At other times, you'll be talking about a particular image and your partner will be relating something entirely *different*. At still other times, one of you will come up with an image, and the other will act as a reinforcing helper. It doesn't matter whether your images are in sync; what matters is the increased excitement and fun you'll be sharing. So dare to be open and vulnerable and let your voices spin out your visions.

Some of you may be having recurring images that make you feel uncomfortable because they never seem to vary. For some people the same images pop up over and over during their practice sessions in the PLEASURE PROCESS.

Frank, a 38-year-old insurance salesman, expressed some concern in group about *his* recurring images.

Everyone here has been sharing all sorts of different images they have during sex. It seems like every time anyone here starts making love, new images come up for them.

For me, it's always the same. Since I've been taking this class, every time my wife and I have sex, the only thing that enters my head is accidentally opening the door and walking in on my mother nude. Now that I hear everyone else having such a variety of images, I think there's something wrong with me because I just keep playing that same one.

When Frank shared this in group, several of the other members began to identify with him and explained that they, too, kept repeating the same image. Some of them explained that after a while the replay of their images had had an interesting effect in that, although the image itself had eventually faded away, the sensuality that it originally released had kept increasing. Here's how Brenda explained this:

Whenever I shared my images with my boyfriend, it was always the same: I kept seeing my brother's penis bulging through his swim trunks. Time after time while we were having sex I kept flashing onto my brother's penis in those same shorts, and I thought I'd never stop.

As I look back now I realize that I never think of my brother anymore during sex. Somehow I've played it all out. I'm through with my work with him—but the orgasms his image initiated keep coming now without him. Now I just think about myself and I enjoy my boyfriend and the orgasms keep flowing.

DISTURBING IMAGES

Occasionally patients come up with images that shock them. These are memories that have been totally blocked out of their awareness and that deal with irresponsible behavior by important adults from their childhoods. Here is an incident that Anne, a beautician in my Monday night group, shared:

When my husband and I were having sex over the weekend, and we were both sharing erotic images from childhood, he was talking about how he had tried to get his penis inside of his older sister when he was a little boy and they were playing. I was talking about how excited I was about what he was saying when I flashed on my father, holding my feet together when I was just an infant. He had an erection, and he was moving my little body, with my legs crossed together, up and down over his penis. His penis came through my legs at just midpoint between my crotch and my knees because my legs were so small. He used the friction of my thighs to stimulate himself and ejaculate.

I had totally blocked out this image, and even though I'm filled with disgust at my father's irre-

sponsible behavior, when my husband and I were having sex and I flashed on this image I broke into a flood of orgasms.

I understand now why often in our sexual play I get such a big kick out of closing my thighs around my husband's erection and watching the head of his penis peep over the opening between my legs.

Anne's story prompted Diane, who is 25 years old and an elementary school teacher, to remember this:

Something similar happened to me, Anne. When my husband George and I were having intercourse I remembered playing in my grandfather's room. He used to babysit with me while my mother worked. Everyone thought he was the fool of the family, but I loved him because he was the only one who had time for me. My mother and father both got up before I did and went to work, and I was usually put to bed at night before they came home.

The only time I ever saw my parents was on Sunday, and then they had so many chores to do in the house and garden that they rarely interacted with me even then.

It was Grandpa who was my playmate. Now that I look back I realize how irresponsible he was because almost every day part of our "play material" was my grandfather's penis. He would take his penis out and tell me how to stroke it and hold it. I was only three then, but somehow just touching his penis made me feel safe.

*When I first brought this up to George, I was a
little frightened to talk about it because the idea of
a grandfather forcing a child to gratify him in that
way is so repulsive to me now. But yet as I talked
to George, that night was the first time in my life
that I had so many orgasms. About fourteen. Normally, I would have fourteen orgasms in two
years!!*

A child is not at fault when a parent is mentally or
emotionally disturbed. Unfortunately many of my patients have reported that their parents approached them
in sexual encounters when they were small. Where this
has occurred, in every case I have found that the child
is desperately abused emotionally and suffers severe ego
damage. But the child is not to blame for the grossly
inappropriate behavior of a sick and irresponsible
parent.

Every child needs the love and affection of a parent,
even when the parent is grossly disturbed. The child is
too small to assess whether the parent's behavior is
healthy. When the parent initiates a kind of interaction
which the child knows is bad, or "sinful," typically the
child will cooperate rather than risk the loss of the
parent's love and approval.

It is normal for a child to want to be stroked and
petted by the parent, and when the parent insists that
this occur in a sexual context, the approval-seeking
child is forced to comply. When patients finally admit to
me that they have engaged in sexual activity with a
parent or relative, I help them understand that they are
not to blame, that children *must listen* to their parents
and that the onus of responsibility is on the parent. Fur-
thermore, regardless of what society says is "good" or
"bad," receiving the total focus of a parent's attention
is what a child longs and works for.

When these FORBIDDEN incestual images finally re-surface into awareness—whether they are real or imag-ined—they tend to be highly erotic. And when they can be removed from the subconscious, the guilt associated with the early experience will have an opportunity to diminish and the person will experience relief and be at peace.

Sometimes the suppressed guilt of an incestuous in-teraction with a parent can be so damaging that it can result in almost total sexual dysfunction. This was true for Celia, who worked in the book section of a local department store.

When she first began in therapy with me, Celia tear-fully explained that although she was 37, she was still a virgin. She enjoyed necking and petting with men, but whenever things progressed further and approached in-tercourse, she panicked and stopped.

After several sessions Celia began to tell me about flashes she was getting when she was necking with a man. In every case these flashes related to her sixth-birthday party and a white organdy dress she had worn. I urged her not to keep these images to herself, but to get them out and to share them verbally with the man she was with. While she was too frightened to do this, she was able to stop dismissing the images, and for the first time she allowed them to unravel in her mind dur-ing the petting and necking.

What appeared in her memory was that her father had lain on top of her after her little friends had left the party. When he had gotten up, her pretty white birthday dress had been all wet in front.

We discussed the possibility that her father had ejacu-lated on top of her and that the guilt of the entire ex-perience had so repelled her, she had been too fright-ened as an adult to relive the experience in any way with another man.

After many months of supportive therapy Celia was able to have intercourse for the first time. As long as this material was repressed, Celia was crippled emotionally and sexually, unable to engage in normal sexual behavior. Once she was able to allow her images to play themselves out in her head, and then share them with me, eventually she was able to share them with her partner. Through this process of getting the images out and allowing them to live openly and freely in the real world, she was finally able to look at them more realistically and realize she wasn't responsible for her father's cruel and despicable behavior.

For Celia, reexperiencing the repressed material was far less painful than experiencing a lifetime of being unable to function sexually as other women do.

I have found with most patients that the disturbing images that occur are rare and that regardless of their content, when they are released, increased sexual freedom results. The *more* material you can get out, the *less* guilt you'll experience and the *more* sensuality you'll enjoy.

Relieve Yourself of Old Guilts

You too are filled with guilts that were implanted in your unconscious when you were very young. I'm always amazed to discover, when I regress patients in hypnosis, that even an infant of four or five months can suffer sexual repression. Something as subtle as removing a child's hands from his or her genitals, or a disapproving grunt from a parent, can be embedded in the subconscious and serve as a punishment which hampers sexual expression in adult life. So many of the patients I treat have suffered this type of repression.

By reliving these events and allowing them to resurface, you can discover how harmless they will seem today.

By letting your images flow, you will be unburdened of your guilt. Once you are free of these guilts, many of your sexual anxieties and inhibitions will disappear. This will allow your feelings of self-worth and self-acceptance to emerge and develop. You will find increased motivation and sex will become a much more positive experience for you.

REDESIGNING OLD EQUATIONS

Steve and Karen had been married for four years. They had had a good relationship during the first year when they had lived with her parents. Although they had very little privacy, because the walls were thin and relatives were always in the house, they had frequent and enjoyable sex. However, once they moved into their own apartment, Steve started suffering from recurring episodes of impotency.

It seemed as if he could perform sexually only under unusual or stressful conditions. He was sure to become erect when they were petting in a movie, making it in a neighbor's swimming pool, going off into the bushes at a party, or necking in the garage of their condominium. But in their own bed he had difficulty becoming aroused.

Karen felt inadequate because he rarely wanted to have sex with her under normal conditions. Steve, on the other hand, was certain something was wrong with *him*. So in order to reassure himself and "prove" his virility, he engaged in "quickies" with his help in the office, or one-night stands at conventions. As long as the circumstances were dangerous, he could perform very well.

The marriage was deteriorating when Steve and Karen first came to me. 'The therapy moved slowly, because, while Karen looked forward to each session, Steve was reluctant to share his personal problems with a stranger. He felt uncomfortable and anxious—especially when our discussions centered on their sexual experiences during childhood.

For the first few sessions Steve seemed so annoyed and so resistant to therapy that Karen was afraid he would quit coming. He made it clear that he was just accommodating her: "This therapy bullshit is a waste of time and money. I want to know that if I had a choice, I'd never do it." But because it meant so much to Karen, Steve kept coming.

Then one night when they were doing their PLEASURE PROCESS homework, a vague image popped into his head. As Karen was fingertipping his back, Steve saw something red. It lasted for a moment, then faded, but . . . he got an erection!

In subsequent sessions more flashes appeared to him: part of a breast; a towel rubbing his genitals; the shape of female genitalia pressing against a tight pair of slacks.

Finally one night he pieced together an entire incident. He was nine years old and Annie, a buxom Swedish au pair the family had brought back from Europe, was taking care of him. Annie was bending over, giving him a bath. He could see part of her breasts. She was wearing a tight, low-cut red blouse.

Every afternoon when he had returned from baseball practice, hot and sweaty, Annie had insisted that Steve strip off his dirty clothes and take a bath. She would run the water, testing it with her elbow until it was just right.

Steve would step in, and the delicious ritual would begin. Annie would scrub each part of his body, slowly and painstakingly. Then, smiling, she'd hand him the soap and tell him to take care of himself "down there."

Afterwards I would stand up and Annie would dry me with a towel. As she brushed over my genitals, it felt wonderful! My thing would get hard.

Then she'd move away and clean off the grimy tub rings. While her back was turned I would play with myself. I would rub myself as fast as I could before she could turn around. I was terrified she'd catch me, but it was a great feeling.

As Steve talked to Karen about his erotic memory, his penis became harder and harder. For the first time in a long while, there were no concerns about his impotency. He was able to maintain his erection and enjoy intercourse with Karen—all under conditions that were *not* stressful or dangerous.

When Steve worked on this experience during their session with me, he was able to understand the connection he had made as a child:

DANGER = EXCITEMENT = ERECTION.

In his nine-year-old mind he had developed the idea that having an erection and playing with himself was wrong and could only happen under shameful conditions. It wasn't a *normal* thing to do under *normal* circumstances.

During his work on the PLEASURE PROCESS Steve was able to redesign the old equation. He realized that it was okay for him to have had an erection when he was being bathed and rubbed by the maid, that it *was* stimulating. When he reexamined this incident as an adult, he accepted that his reactions were normal. His adult understanding enabled him to remove the guilt and the FOR-

BIDDEN labels that he had long ago attached to this early erotica. He was then able to formulate a new equation:

NORMAL CONDITIONS = EXCITEMENT = ERECTION.

By giving himself license to have enjoyed those sensual feeling with Annie, Steve was able to give himself permission to let these erotic feelings flow into healthy sexual excitement with his wife.

New Heights of Eroticism

The differences in the variety, content and quality of the images that can emerge are endless.

You may laugh and talk about you as a little girl running down the halls of your grammar school, while your partner's voice may join in suggesting he'd like to catch you and pull your pants down.

Or, you may just as easily veer off on different tangents, one partner talking about caressing the soft, wrinkled face of a grandfather, while the other's voice is wandering through a beautiful pastoral countryside.

Start to unlock those childhood images and share them verbally with your partner. This will allow you to make contact with your original erotic child—the sensuality you knew before it was contaminated by society's standards and "don'ts."

There are, however, two important cautions that may limit your verbal behavior during lovemaking: avoid discussing actual sexual experiences that you had after the age of twelve; also avoid discussing contemporary sexual fantasies, if you have any about other men. This kind of talk is destructive. It will hurt your partner and create distance.

What we are looking for in the PROCESS is an increased ability to share sensual experiences that occurred before your teenage years, as well as early fantasies. Whatever childhood images come into your head during sex, *share them* with your partner. As you both share your images, new heights of eroticism will be reached.

Chapter 11

Step V:
Your Loving License

Take it, girl! And fear no after,
Take your fill of all this laughter.

—RICHARD LE GALLIENNE

In the phase I call YOUR LOVING LICENSE, for the first time in the PLEASURE PROCESS the equal sharing stops. The complete focus turns toward you. A Loving License is given to you. All sexual play is concentrated on your body *alone*. Your breasts, clitoris, vagina and other erogenous zones are stimulated both by you *and* by your partner. *There is no attention directed to his body; there is no contact yet with his genitalia.* At this point, by completely giving to you he is putting erotic markers in the bank for himself, for withdrawal later.

As in the first two steps of the PLEASURE PROCESS, give yourself at least 15 minutes for Step V.* Before you begin, you need to recycle the entire PROCESS back to Step I. That is, you will do Step I, HUGGING, for 15 minutes, then go to Step II, FINGERTIPPING, for another 15 minutes. As you proceed, remember to verbalize and

---

* Although I don't expect you to use a stopwatch during sex, I'm suggesting these time segments to give you an idea of how leisurely the PROCESS unfolds.

share your erotic childhood images, then you'll be ready to start this step, YOUR LOVING LICENSE.

In the earlier steps, you learned how to switch off your thinking mind, stop all the negative tapes, and use your natural sensuality, as uncontaminated as it was when you vere very small. You have already been programmed to focus on your own body. By using this training, you will now be able to fall even deeper into your feelings.

There's no holding back. The spotlight is on you. Your partner becomes the musician, playing your body as if it were a precious instrument. He has the opportunity to feel totally in command. Perhaps for the first time in his life, he is in complete control. You will feel appreciated, happy and adored.

Everything he does is "right," because in this step he is devoted solely to pleasuring you. You accept all the pleasure . . . experience being cared for . . . receive all his gestures. You take it all in, for yourself.

In this step, the man begins by kissing and caressing your body. His focus is on enjoying your breasts. For the first part of this step he should purposely avoid your vagina, spending at least a full ten minutes pleasuring your breasts, massaging your body, and kissing you.

There is a direct psychological, as well as physiological, wiring from the breasts to the vagina. When you can think about your breasts and all the delightful sensations you are experiencing—really focus into your sensory receptors—you will find that your vagina will start throbbing and contracting in a subtle rhythm. These are your magical push muscles. They are being gently signaled to awakening as your breasts are stimulated.

It's time now to push out on these muscles—out and in—out and in. Push out firmly. Concentrate on every movement as your body stirs to life.

Notice how good your breasts feel as you do this. Take your hand and feel your enlarged, sensitized nipples.

> Your entire body can blossom now into a
> sensual grid.

Because of his training in the PROCESS, your partner is able to enjoy all the responses that he is capable of evoking in you. His attitude, his body language and his verbal observations are totally approving and nonjudgmental. This acceptance encourages you to tune directly into your own body . . . no cross-wiring into old tapes and FORBIDDEN signs. The "musts," "shoulds," and negative equations of childhood disappear. They melt away.

When the foreplay is slow and loving, your mind reassures your vagina: all is well. You are being loved and cared for in a safe and trusting environment. This message is the key to an emotional license, allowing your vagina to loosen up, lubricate and prepare for penetration later.

As you become aroused by all this loving attention to your breasts, allow yourself to let go. You're a creative woman now, savoring all your primitive richness as you bear down on your magical push muscles, as if you were trying to push them out of your body. It is the same sensation as trying to urinate. But you're a big girl now, and you won't. Instead, you'll intensify your erotic vaginal sensations and increase the probability of multiorgasmic responses.

Everything opens up, emotionally and physically. All the restrictions about your early learning, your dos and don'ts, are dismissed. All the controls are forgotten. You, the female, can trust yourself.

The woman who pursues what is pleasurable for herself while maintaining a sensitivity to the needs of her partner invites the partner to abandon himself, too (especially his "spectatoring" self), and let go more freely. According to Drs. Raymond Babineau and Allan J. Schwartz, "a partner who is relatively free of performance anxiety helps to reciprocally induce an atmosphere of confidence and spontaneity."[16]

This is what happens in YOUR LOVING LICENSE.

After at least 10 minutes of caressing your breasts and your body, your partner's hands and mouth can now move down to your genitals.

For many of you, your ready vagina will orgastically convulse at his touch. You will be surprised to see how easily your orgasms will flow out. Others will find this a highly passionate *pre*-orgastic phase.

Keep in mind that while you're involved in this step, you're also incorporating all the steps you've learned so far. So be ready to invite your erotic child to come into play. Share your images with your partner. When you do, you will find that the adding on of each additional step to the one you're practicing at the moment will serve to enhance your total experience. Here's how it worked for this couple.

JASMINE'S HOT "MAN-BABY"

Mark and Jasmine, high-school sweethearts, had been married for 10 years. They were both still very much in love, but their sex life had grown mechanical and infrequent. In fact, Jasmine usually avoided sex because she so rarely had an orgasm, she was reluctant even to get started. Instead she focused most of her attention on a small dog-grooming business she had developed.

One evening Mark complained bitterly that she was never home at night—that she was married to her business, not to him:

You touch those damn poodles more than you touch me! We never have sex anymore, and if we do, you're more like a robot than a woman.

Well, that's not good enough for me. I want more of you . . . more time . . . more sex . . . more everything, or I'm getting out.

The next day Jasmine called my office for an appointment. They both came in to see me for conjoint therapy, and the work on repairing their marriage began. As part of their therapy I introduced them to the PLEASURE PROCESS.

They had been practicing the first three steps for about three weeks when a major breakthrough occurred for them. It was on a Sunday afternoon when they were having sex. Mark was kissing her breasts when an image appeared: he flashed back and saw himself as an infant in his mother's arms. Suddenly, it was *her* breasts he was sucking. Remembering his PLEASURE PROCESS steps, he began to share his images, whimpering in a soft, babylike voice:

Mommy, this is my breast, I need it. I get to suck it all. It's just for me, 'cause I'm so little.

As Mark continued, Jasmine found herself getting caught up in the frenzy of his excitement:

Yes, baby dear, you're my precious baby. Keep sucking, love . . . you're making your mommy very hot.

Jasmine explained to me during our next meeting that seeing Mark so completely involved in enjoying her breasts was a tremendous turn-on for her. Just watching the intensity of his passion had caused her, for the first time, to orgasm *without* any vaginal stimulation. She hadn't believed it was possible to become that aroused by breast stimulation alone:

I can't believe how natural and easy it all was. When Mark started talking and sucking my breasts that way, I guessed what was happening to him and I loved it! I loved the idea of this hot man-baby on top of me. I got all mixed up in my own incestuous fantasies and really got into it. I didn't start thinking, like I usually do, about what was "nice" or "good" or "right"—all that judgmental junk that you've been telling us was stopping our sensuality. You were right. When I stopped all the negative labels and just went with my natural feelings, it was terrific!

We both feel like kids, now. We can hardly believe all the fun we're having staying home nights! It's like discovering a new play toy!!

Kinsey observed that about two percent of women are capable of having an orgasm through breast or other nongenital stimulation. Using the PLEASURE PROCESS, I find that *most* of my patients are able to orgasm through nongenital stimulation after just a few months of practicing the steps.

As *you* continue to practice the PLEASURE PROCESS your orgasmic responses will increase in frequency, duration, and intensity. Eventually you will be able to achieve multi-orgasms . . . perhaps even the *maxi-orgasm.* *

As the multi-orgasmic female, you will feel wonderful, self-confident and loving. One of my patients wrote the following love note to her partner, describing her experience in this step:

> *I couldn't do it by myself. I needed you. You accepted whatever I said or did. In your arms I felt so free . . . so lovely.*

> *You weren't judgmental or critical. I always felt adorable the way you appreciated me so and encouraged me to go on.*

> *You gave me a loving license.*

> *When you smiled . . . when you looked at me the way you did, I felt safe.*

> *I was willing to try anything. I never felt ridiculous when I made strange movements or noises. I could do or say whatever came into my head; unrelated images, erotic fantasies, even baby talk. I felt exciting and sensual.*

> *With you, I exploded with all sorts of extravagant creations and inventions. All my deeply hidden secrets erupted. I never dared to experience so much before.*

---

* See Chapter 13, "101 Orgasms"

When we made love, I wanted your interest, your caring . . . and I got it, freely and willingly from you.

You seemed so happy when we were very close.

I couldn't have made it by myself. The freedom I found in our lovemaking was the fuel that spurred me on.

It was my Loving License.

Chapter 12

Step VI:
The Loving Experience

One turf shall serve as pillow for us both;
One heart, one bed, two bosoms and one troth.

—SHAKESPEARE

During this step, the LOVING EXPERIENCE, your partner's attention turns back to himself. He has just finished an entire sequence in Step V of pleasuring *you*.
Now it's time for him to concentrate totally on himself
and enjoy his first penetration of the PLEASURE PRO-
CESS. Having spent a sequence helping you to get in
touch with all your erotic senses, it's his turn now. It's
time for your partner to withdraw his markers. It's time
for him to focus on his *own* pleasurable feelings as he
enters you in whichever position he prefers and sex, the
elixir, the core fiber weaving the link between man and
woman, begins.

Perhaps no human experience comes closer to a
union with universal consciousness than intercourse
with a loving other. It is the peak, the culmination of
one of life's most exciting, satisfying, and often awe-
inspiring gifts. And part of the gift of this experience is
orgasm—one of the most natural transitory endow-
ments we can claim—where we can shift from animal
to man to God.

Again and again we strive for orgasm. For some of us, it is the ultimate experience—skyrockets exploding. For others, orgasm is a small match lit to ward off the darkness of a dismal existence. And there are many people who are unable to experience orgasm at all. These people are burdened by such overwhelming repression, that even in the PLEASURE PROCESS they will require considerable time to become orgasmic.

Customarily, in sexual intercourse, attention is directed almost entirely to the genital area. Once *penis erectus* is sighted, both partners assume that penetration should occur immediately. They worry that otherwise the erection will disappear. This fear results in hurried and unfulfilling sex.

In the PLEASURE PROCESS both partners learn to enjoy themselves regardless of the turgidity, flaccidity, or degree of lubrication of their genitals. The man's erotic experience is no longer ruled by the erection of his penis, because during the first two steps, HUGGING and FINGERTIPPING, it doesn't matter whether he's erect. Perhaps for the first time in his life he has the opportunity to concentrate on his emotional, rather than his physical, self. Until this sixth step, no attention whatsoever has been directed toward his penis, so there has been no occasion to perform. He has the freedom to forget about his partner, forget about foreplay, forget about performance, and forget about erections.

He has been able to enjoy getting into his feelings. For the male in this PROCESS, sex is no longer a race to get it up, get it in, and get it over with before he feels inadequate.

In Step V, your partner focuses on *you*, issuing a "Loving License" to you. He helps you to explore the depths of your sensuality. And it's contagious!

He knows he is the author of your joy. In this sixth step, he feels enormously confident as intercourse begins. He has a partner who is happy with all the loving attention and fun she's enjoyed. She is feeling completely willing and receptive. He knows he is already a success. And because he's already succeeded in pleasing her, *there's no way he can fail!*

His sense of mastery is so satisfying it crowns him with an aura of pride. His body becomes erotically magnetized so that he attracts some of *your* energy and excitement and adds it to his own sexual feelings.

So much of him feels alive because he has become more intensely sensitized by the waiting. He experiences sensations in parts of his body that never before felt erotic: toes, fingers, back, face . . . most of his skin. With his entire body responding this way, it becomes apparent to him that his erection is not the only agent of his sensuality—his penis is not the only thing he's got going for him.

Knowing this, he's not as anxious or concerned about getting and maintaining an erection . . . and without this anxiety, it becomes easier for him to move naturally into an erect state.

He feels powerful, like a king!

Gone are anxieties about the tyranny of performance: *no more worries* about who orgasms first . . . *no more worries* about scorekeeping . . . *no more worries* about impotence . . . *no more worries* about premature ejaculation.

He doesn't have to worry about being soft or hard or pleasing because you are already lost in the passion of the PROCESS. He can more fully attend to himself and experience his *own* passion.

Where time stops its blazing pace.

Where together you expand your territories, sharing all your positive feelings and images.

Where together you say or do or think whatever
you want.

Where cloistered in the blanket of each other's arms
you enter into an intoxicating, dreamlike euphoria, losing touch with reality, sometimes even hallucinating
happy, poignant scenes. It's a druglike state where
couples, intertwined, float . . . weightless and brakeless.

Sharing deeper and fuller orgasms, you will both feel
the magnitude of your emotional and physical connection. It's an oral and tactile extravaganza, where his and
your orgasms turn into "ours." You each maximize
your own excitement, while reveling in the happiness
of the other's pleasure. Genuine one-on-one intimacy is
achieved when you join together in this ultimate LOVING
EXPERIENCE.

I am utterly content
In all my spirit is no ripple of unrest
For I have opened unto you the wide gates of my being
And like a tide you have flowed into me.

—EUNICE TIETJENS

PART THREE:

MORE TREASURES

Chapter 13

101
Orgasms

Yea, to such freshness, fairness, fullness,
fineness, freeness
Yea, to such surging, swaying, sighing,
swelling, shrinking
Yea, to such bodings, broodings, beatings,
blanchings, blessings
Yea to such rashness, ratherness, rareness,
ripeness, richness

—THOMAS HARDY

One of the most common questions I hear from my female patients when they first enter therapy is, "Dr. Kassorla, I'd like to have an orgasm every time we have sex. Is this too much to expect?"

My answer is very much the same each time. "Of course not," I tell them. "In fact, you can have dozens! If you want to . . . you can have as many as 101 orgasms."*

Whenever I discuss the amazing potential of the female orgasmic response with these patients, they react in the same way: "What! 101 orgasms in one night! That's physically impossible. You must be joking!"

---

* The number "101" is not given as a computer figure or numerical quotient that must be realized. But it is a pleasurable reality that is being achieved by many of my patients.

Before you throw this book down in disbelief, let me assure you that it *is* possible, and possible for *you*. A woman is capable of having orgasms for hours, and need stop only when she is totally satisfied.

I first began treating anorgastic females in Britain in 1967. My interest then was in offering these patients the kind of information and education that would enable them to experience themselves as normally functioning sexual females. My concern was to help them achieve orgasm. For most of them, after so many years of dysfunction, a single orgasm, even at irregular intervals, would have been considered a satisfactory measure of success.

Little did I dream at that time that my methodologies would form the basis of a PROCESS that would enable the women who practiced it to enjoy dozens and dozens of orgasms, easily and pleasurably whenever they wanted. Looking back, I never would have believed that this was physically possible or even desirable. But I know now that the potential for a continuing stream of easy, almost involuntary orgasmic responses clearly exists. And what is even more remarkable is that multi-orgasmic responsivity can be had with so little effort. It is not something you and your partner will strive to achieve. Rather, it is something that will happen to you as a natural consequence of the PLEASURE PROCESS.

Increased Sensuality Offers Increased Safety

Contrary to popular belief, increased sensuality offers increased safety to a relationship. As a woman becomes more sensual, she will feel more confident with herself and safer in the relationship.

Before practicing the PLEASURE PROCESS experience, many male patients report they are worried that the sexually free woman will neglect her responsibilities, become promiscuous and never stay home. They are frightened that their wives will leave as soon as their full sexual potential is unleashed. They fear they'll become notorious for their sexual prowess, want to copulate incessantly, and start patroling the local pubs for prospects. Actually the reverse happens.

Women who learn to orgasm for hours, until total satiation, become grateful and more loving with their men. They want to be near them, because their lovers are the source of their unending joy.

In the PLEASURE PROCESS a mutual dependency starts to grow that acts as a healthy glue, bonding the partners together. A stability and longevity develop that can come only with this kind of sharing and interdependency. The steps of the PROCESS are so rewarding that the partners realize that no other relationship can compare or can offer them this deep sense of comfort and security. No other relationship will result in the feelings of personal pride and self-acceptance *both* of them will enjoy.

This is especially true for women. Research findings validate this. Many scientific studies have found that women who are sensual and orgasm more frequently, tend also to be more successful, more motivated in their work, and are more able to express feelings of heightened self-worth and self-esteem.

In the PLEASURE PROCESS there is so much joy in feeling connected that both partners experience a sense of safety as fears of being rejected decrease and mutual pleasure increases. Arguments become shorter as the improved communication skills generalize to situations outside the bedroom.

What Is an Orgasm?

What is the big "O"? Is there a "right" kind? A "good" or a "standard" orgasm? If you think these questions can be answered easily, ask your friends. Each one will probably give you a very different, highly personalized response. Believe all of them, because an orgasm is a *subjective* experience.

Anaïs Nin described it this way: "Electric flesh-arrows . . . traversing the body. A rainbow of color strikes the eyelids. A foam of music falls over the ears. It is the gong of the orgasm."

Wilhelm Reich used the term *orgasm* "in a very special sense to refer to the complete surrender to sexual excitation with the total involvement of the body in the convulsive movements of discharge . . . an ecstatic experience."[17] Joseph and Lois Bird, in *Sexual Loving,* declare "it is the ultimate psychophysical act in the drama of sexual love."

Freud referred to orgasm as the pleasure that results from the release of body tension. He related the degree of one's pleasure to the degree of tension released: the greater the degree of your orgastic discharge, the more rapid your release, and the greater your pleasure.

Some authorities describe orgasm as a reflex action, a natural body happening much like coughing, laughing or sneezing.

One of my patients explained her orgasms to me as delicious convulsive feelings that seem to take over her entire body:

Everything else stops—the world goes on hiatus as my body becomes my life.

A tingly hot feeling slowly spreads all over me—
from head to toe. It gets more and more important.

All I can think about is my vagina.
The whole world becomes my vagina.
I just hang on.
I'm helpless to stop it . . . and I don't want to.

Every touch seems to penetrate deep inside of me.

I'm sometimes frightened but I keep going with the
gorgeous feelings.

Soon my orgasms come tumbling out. Then they
stop, and I feel so happy and so quiet.

Then my husband starts again . . . gently playing
with my clit. His fingers push into my vagina,
then back again to my clit—and zap! It all starts
happening again.

I can't think. All I can do is feel.

Masters and Johnson, in their monumental scientific
contribution, *Human Sexual Response,* have researched
in amazing detail the physiology of the orgasm. They
suggest that orgasm can be divided into four significant
phases: the *excitement phase,* involving stimulation or
foreplay; the *plateau phase,* involving continuation of
stimulation, or the building up of a charge or tension;
the *orgasmic phase,* representing maximum sexual tension; and the *resolution phase,* during which the individual returns through plateau and excitement levels to
an unstimulated state. *(See Figure 1.)*

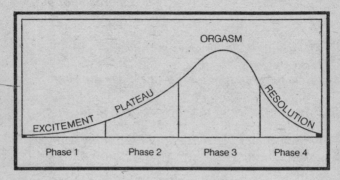

Figure 1. The four phases of the orgasm.

Your Orgastic Continuum

The four phases of the Masters and Johnson model demonstrate what typically occurs when sex terminates in orgasm. In the PLEASURE PROCESS this commonly accepted four-stage progression is dramatically extended to include a concept that I call the *orgastic continuum.*

This new concept is very simple. What occurs in the PLEASURE PROCESS is that the popular four-phase model is modified to allow for continuing orgasms. With highly orgastic females, Phase 4 (resolution) becomes a transitory resting stage before the onset of the next orgasm . . . and the next . . . and the next . . . and the next. The level of excitation does *not* diminish and the orgasmic releases do *not* subside until you are completely happy, ready and satisfied. *(See Figure 2.)*

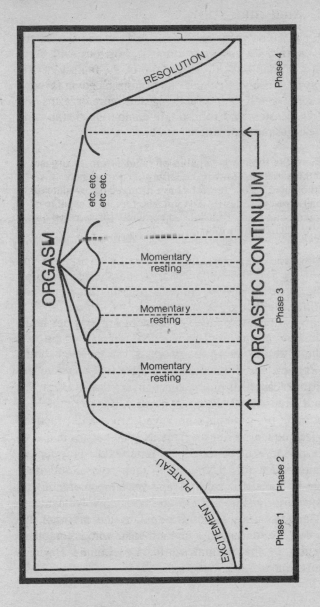

Figure 2. The Orgastic Continuum.

Even if you've never before had an orgasm, in the PLEASURE PROCESS your orgastic horizons will seem endless. You'll make a reality out of the fantasy of 101 orgasms. Once you've had one orgasm by going through the steps, you'll keep practicing and more orgasms will follow. Masters and Johnson, in comparing "female and male orgasmic expression," state:

> First, the female is capable of rapid return to orgasm immediately following an orgasmic experience, if re-stimulated before tensions have dropped below plateau-phase response levels. Second, the female is capable of maintaining an orgasmic experience for a relatively long period of time.[18]

Now you can get ready for as many orgasms as you want! As psychiatrist Dr. Mary Jane Sherfey explains, "The intensity of the multiple orgasms do not abate until fatigue of the responding muscles has set in."[19] A healthy woman can have 50 or more orgasms per hour, and can continue until exhaustion. She can go on . . . and on . . . and on. In the PROCESS, this muscle exhaustion typically occurs some time after two hours of delightful pleasure in going through the steps. Does this sound impossible?

Among the patients who have learned and practiced my techniques, having as many as 100 orgasms in a two-hour period is not uncommon. Afterwards, they report, they're better able to focus into their normal activities. They feel peaceful, relaxed, and yet more energetic and ready to participate in work and family involvements.

The PLEASURE PROCESS explodes the myth of the neurotic and deranged nymphomaniac who is unable to function in the normal world. Dr. Lonnie Barbach reports that:

Recent research by Arvalea Nelson indicates that consistently orgasmic women tend to describe themselves as contented, good-natured, insightful, self-confident, independent, realistic, strong, capable, and understanding while nonorgasmic women tend to describe themselves as bitter, despondent, dissatisfied, distrustful, fussy, immature, inhibited, prejudiced, and sulky.[20]

In the PLEASURE PROCESS a woman can enjoy an active, vital life and still experience the orgastic continuum of seemingly endless orgasms, when she wishes, as a natural part of her sexuality.

The difference between the mere satisfaction of one or two orgasms and the satiation of 101 orgasms is more than a question of numbers. The distinction between satisfaction and satiation is one of the cornerstones that supports and defines the PLEASURE PROCESS.

Why be satisfied with one or two orgasms? In learning this PROCESS, a healthy woman can enjoy repeated orgasms for as long as she wants to. "The more orgasms a woman has, the stronger they become; the more orgasms she has, the more she *can* have."[21] [Italics added.]

There is a great difference between satisfaction and satiation. Your body is capable of experiencing more and more pleasure . . . more and more orgasms . . . until you simply don't *want* any more. This is the meaning of satiation.

But don't get caught up in the numbers game. The figure "101" is not meant to serve as a goal for all women, although, in fact, you may exceed it; "101" is merely a symbol for the number of orgasms that will satiate *you*. For some women this may mean 2 to 20, for others it will be over 60, while still others will want to enjoy hours of orgasms.

Unfortunately, women all over the world believe that

they *should be satisfied* with one good orgasm. This kind of nonsensical prattle has been handed down from generation to generation, resulting in centuries of misinformation about female sexuality. We've been conditioned to believe that one intense orgasm should bring "full satisfaction," act as a strong sedative, and alleviate sexual tension for several days to come. This is simply fallacious.

This notion doesn't hold up in terms of physiological reality. Each orgasm a woman has is followed by a prompt refilling of what is called the "venous erectile chambers." Then a circular situation occurs, resulting in tissue tension in these chambers. Because of the engorgement and swelling that follows, a physical need for relief is set into motion.* Only an orgasm can offer this relief. But once the second orgasm occurs, there is another prompt refilling of the venous erectile chambers, more engorgement and swelling, more tissue tension, and a continuing desire for another orgasm. *(See Figures 3 and 4.)*

And so, physically speaking, a normal woman can have orgasm after orgasm until satiation occurs. When this happens, she will have complete psychological and physiological satisfaction. Then she can bask in the dignity of feeling totally adequate, healthy and feminine.

The Maxi-Orgasm

Occasionally in the literature of sexual therapy you will encounter a supposedly unusual and exotic phenomenon called the *maxi*-orgasm. It is said that the *maxi* is so

---

* This is similar to the relief needed when there is tissue tension in the bladder.

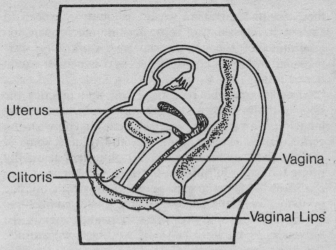

Figure 3. Female organs and tissue as they appear under normal conditions.

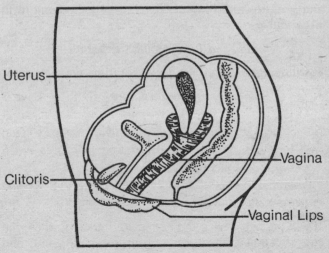

Figure 4. Female organs and tissue as they appear during sexual arousal.

rare, so unobtainable, women shouldn't expect to achieve it. This kind of sensually limiting propaganda infuriates me! The women who have worked on their sexuality with me know that the *maxi* is neither exotic nor unusual.

Most of you who read this book and practice the steps of the PLEASURE PROCESS will learn to enjoy having two or three dozen orgasms whenever you wish. As your orgasms increase in intensity and volume, some of you will move on to an even higher plateau of sensuality where the happy surprise of the *maxi* will occur.

Just as its name implies, the *maxi*-orgasm is big . . . *gigantic* . . . totally engrossing and totally compelling. When you have one you will understand what A. B. Stevenson meant when he said, "And bells were struck that never rang in churches."

The *maxi* is the pinnacle of a complete physiological and psychological release. No other sexual experience can compete with the *maxi* in terms of the issuing forth of primitive, pure erotica.

The maxi is the infinite orgasm.

It will happen to those of you who allow yourselves to:

—*get caught up* in the *involuntary* rhythms of your body;

—whirl with the *pulsating movements* of your vagina;

—let every nerve ending in your pelvic area *reach out* to be touched;

—*immerse* yourself deeply in all the *eruptions* and magnificent spasms.

It will happen during the PLEASURE PROCESS when you can abandon control, leave your thinking mind, and bathe in the sensual magic of your feelings. Then the *maxi* can become a regular part of your sexual repertoire.

During the *maxi* a profusion of warm liquid will erupt from the vagina, a fountain of erotic juices that are tasteless and odorless. Through the use of a clear, phallic-shaped camera which was inserted into the vagina during masturbation, Masters and Johnson learned that most of the vaginal lubricant was actually exuded by the walls of the vagina in a process similar to sweating.

Many women become frightened when they feel this rush of liquid spilling out of their vaginas. They fear they are urinating. *Stop worrying!* It isn't urine. During the *maxi* there is a prolific production of liquid. Accept and enjoy this erotic flow and your passion will be prolific, too!

One of my patients described this liquid as her "love gusher." The description of Philip G. Brooks, M.D., a noted Beverly Hills gynecologist, is somewhat more formal:

> During pre-orgasmic excitation of the female . . . the production of vaginal lubrication arises from the vaginal epithileum with a transudation of the mucoid material directly from the cellular lining of the vagina.
>
> In experiments by Masters and Johnson, it is noted that the mucoid material is the result of marked dilation of the blood vessels within the lining of the entire vagina.
>
> The vasocongestion that results from stimulation can produce a copious amount of mucoid material.

The sensations and convulsive experiences of the *maxi* are similar to those of regular orgasms, except that they feel deeper, more concentrated and more intense. Sometimes my patients report that they think they will "burst"—or "come unglued"—during the *maxi*. What actually happens is a rapturous elongation of the orgastic plateau. They go on and on enjoying their *maxi*, until the sweet, compelling gushers subside.

The *maxi's* are much like an explosion of countless eruptions, with each individual sensation a spasmodic bursting deep inside your vagina, anus and stomach.

Joggers often discuss a state of euphoria that is reached after 20 to 30 minutes of jogging in which their muscles move into an almost involuntary state of action and their legs seem to move without thinking. They express these feelings in terms that sound almost orgastic.

A similar state of involuntary muscle reaction occurs in the *maxi*. That is, after having two or three dozen orgasms the vagina seems to take over by itself and the orgasms occur in a repeated fashion with only moments of rest in between and with little or no stimulation necessary. By merely having your partner behave in an affectionate and fondling manner, without vaginal stimulation or penetration, the *maxi*-orgasms will roll on. Of course, the intensity can certainly be increased by kissing the breasts, or by penetration or clitoral and vaginal manipulation.

Once you reach the *maxi* plateau, which can take over during any phase of the orgasmic cycle, you can continue your sexual play and orgasming for two hours or more, depending upon individual desires, or until total satiation or muscle exhaustion occurs.*

---

* When dealing with female patients who had been involved in the drug culture before therapy, it is not unusual to hear reports of high levels of frequency and intensity in their orgasmic experiences. Women heavily involved in the use of LSD, Quaaludes, and other kinds of drugs report experiencing between 100 to 200 orgasms during a single session of lovemaking.

In the PLEASURE PROCESS I encourage my patients to stay

The experience of the *maxi* is so complete that the entire body becomes caught up in the orgasm. One patient explained her *maxi's* to me in this way:

When I have regular orgasms I can feel the convulsions in my vagina going in and out in an easy, pleasant way. I feel good. The spasms in my vagina are great; they just roll out of me.

Then after a while I have my maxi's *and—wow! It's like a gorgeous dance. I love to watch myself in the mirror. I feel so beautiful . . . and the sight of me in a happy mood is almost overwhelming.*

Sometimes I fantasize I'm a passionate storm as enormous waves of orgasms come crashing over me. Other times I'm a gentle wind swaying along with my orgasms. Then I'm a beautiful Venetian fountain as the streams of water comes flowing out of me.

My entire body seems to swell up. My mouth becomes a vagina . . . my feet and hands have a kind of hot orgasm . . . my eyes, too.

I just cling onto my partner, loving every minute. I bury my mouth and my vagina into him. My stomach heaves up and down. It seems to be having its own orgasms as I go completely out of control.

Oh! It's so wonderful! All I can do is hang on— hooked onto his mast.

---

away from *any* kind of artificial stimulants, including drugs or alcohol, because by following these simple steps, the natural highs of involuntary orgasms and the *maxi* can be reached with ease.

It's everything.
There's nothing else—material things, money, pos-
sessions—nothing else matters.

Each sensation in itself would be enough.
It's an ecstasy too beautiful, too profound to trust
to mere words.

I wish every woman could have it.

You Have a Right!

You have a right to be an orgastic creature.
You have a right to be an erotic human being.
You have a right to be your unique, sensual self.
Whether your orgasm is a gong, a volcanic body tremor, a landslide of tumbling sensations, or a warm bath of caressing melodies, you have a right to be satisfied totally, accepted totally, understood and cared for totally.

I want you to know the exquisite swirl of the *maxi*.
I want you to feel the exotic dance of the "joyous epilepsy."
I want you to experience the untamable *maxi* orgasm.
These are the rights that, as a woman, you inherited at birth; these are the rights that you're finally free to exercise in the PLEASURE PROCESS.

Chapter 14

Romance
of the Soft-On

*After all the erring and meanderings,
impasses and false starts, heroic
enterprises and sweaty efforts—that it
should come to this! And should a man be
able to land on the moon, and worry less
about his return than whether, once
returned, he can satisfy his wife?*

———WOLFGANG LEDERER, M.D.

Let's pause for a moment and consider what happens to
a man when he ejaculates before he feels he has satisfied his partner. His penis becomes limp; it's immobi-
lized. This causes many men to experience shame and a
sense of profound disappointment. They are haunted
by the myth that great lovers have piston-and-pump
genitals and can stroke their ladies to ecstasy with per-
petual hard-ons. Because, traditionally, an erection is
considered to be the sign of a man's virility, the inability
to maintain one as long as he thinks he "should" can be
a deadly blow to his self-esteem.

The Fear of the Soft-On

For many women, too, the soft-on represents only
negative expectations. This condition of the soft penis
signals to a woman that she has been robbed of the

possibility of satisfaction. If her lover ejaculates before she is ready to orgasm, she knows from experience that this means the end of pleasure, the death of intimacy; her joy is over.

Here are some of the comments that my female patients have made which express their feelings of resentment and defeat at this frustrating occurrence:

> When he comes so fast, it's all over before I even warm up. I haven't even got a chance.

> I'd better get mine before he gets his or I'm finished. And if I know I'll never make it, what's the use of even trying? It's getting so that I hate the whole idea of having sex.

> I feel that his coming is the enemy. Once he does, he's through and I never have my orgasm. There's nothing left for me.

For men, the premature soft-on has represented failure, a cause for blame. One of my patients, a 43-year-old cabinetmaker, explained his feelings of fear and inadequacy to me this way.

JIM'S DRILL SERGEANT

> Every time I can't get it up, or I ejaculate prematurely, I feel embarrassed. I start perspiring and I just want to disappear. I fantasize that my wife is an army sergeant in uniform who is barking at me:
>   Hep-two-three-four!
>   Hep-two-three-four!
>   Get it hard!

Push it in!
Hep-two-three-four!
Stick it out!
Strong as iron,
Like a pipe.
Bulging out!
Be a man!
A real man!
Hep-two-three-four!

From what my other male patients tell me, Jim's fantasy about his wife's screaming demands is not too dissimilar from the way they experience the terror of their soft-ons.

Each man hears a different voice, which he believes echoes the cries of all women . . . nightmarish . . . haranguing . . . unrelenting. And in order to quiet this repetitive drone and turn the spotlight away from his genitals, he resorts to diversionary tactics. He complains about anything he can think of: business, money, in-laws, the children or the economy.

The most effective ploy he can use, however, is to direct his complaints at *you*:

—"I wish you'd lose weight."
—"Why can't you take a bath just before we go to bed?"
—"Did you have garlic again for lunch?"

By redirecting the spotlight toward *your* most vulnerable areas, he is able to transfer the burden of his shame and embarrassment to you. Now you're left holding the bag of responsibility for his failure, while he can feel absolved of blame.

Another well-worn diversionary tactic to conceal his feelings of inadequacy is to withdraw into silence or become angry. One of my patients explained that his instinct was to turn over and pretend to fall asleep quickly. By hiding his soft-on from his wife he hoped to avoid further humiliation:

I would lie there in the dark after sex, wondering what was wrong with me because I didn't know how to satisfy her.

This patient suffered the anguish that men have known through the ages: the fear of the wilting erection. For centuries men have been so preoccupied with the pressure to perform that they have forgotten how to abandon themselves to the lovemaking experience. Overburdened with the exhausting job of assuming their masculine roles, they have had little emotional time or energy left for sensuality.

Men have been saddled with unrealistic expectations: prove your manliness . . . be dauntless, fearless and tearless . . . no physical touching . . . shake hands, slap backs.

Men don't have a chance.

Joseph and Lois Bird, again in *Sexual Loving*, explain that by the time he is 13 years old, the male has been indoctrinated with the understanding that he must be the macho jock and never:

1. Embrace other males his own age, older or younger (except his father or close family member—if older— in situations of high emotion).
2. Embrace females other than his mother, and then only on her initiative and when it is inescapable. (Embracing girls may be something he fantasizes but fears initiating.)

He also has learned that:

3. Touching of male peers is to be limited to aggressive acts—hitting, wrestling, etc.—out of fear of being suspected of homosexuality.

4. Nonperson pleasurable touching experiences (intimacy substitutes) are to be strictly limited. Soft, highly sensuous fabrics are not for males. A fur muff or a velvet-collared coat may provide intimacy substitutes for girls, never boys. And this applies as well to sensual touching of self. At a time when girls are learning the benefits (pleasuring) of hand and body lotions, boys are being encouraged to take brisk showers, and to exercise to "toughen up the body."[22]

Feeling soft and vulnerable isn't encouraged in a boy's upbringing. Rather, he's taught to be *un*feeling, *un*sentimental, rugged and aggressive . . . an invincible James Bond figure with a bit of Jehovah thrown in! His job is to produce . . . achieve.

Men have accepted the nonsense of their impoverished inheritance like obedient children. They have silently tolerated and accepted the shackles of the established male image.

In the PLEASURE PROCESS these inhuman criteria of "mucho machismo" are discarded: the male is able to cast off his spectatoring self. He can stop *observing* the action, yours and his. He can say goodbye to *fearing* impotency and premature ejaculation. He can stop *proving* himself with the never-ending "hit-'em-and-run" sex-capades.

King Kong understood. He had no masculine image to prove or to protect. He was clearly stronger and more powerful than the most threatening male. Yet, he knew how to be soft and sentimental. He was gentle and loving, caring and monogamous. He was sexually secure. He could afford to throw away the macho role playing. So can your lover.

The Soft-On Can Be Sensual

The myth that the soft-on is a sign of failure or prohibits sensuality is nonsense. A man can learn that having an orgasm is only part of the total event. It's like the sea. When the tide moves out, you don't feel disappointed because you know it will return. Just as the tide will come back . . . so will another erection.

When both partners can accept the fact that the soft-on is not the enemy, it can become a friend, a helpful addition to a man's sexual equipment. Besides, during the early steps of the PROCESS a woman can learn to have several orgasms, so it doesn't matter how quickly her partner ejaculates. This won't be the critical factor in determining the extent or level of her satisfaction.

As Babineau and Schwartz have explained, "Males have to learn that sexual pleasure is not necessarily 'penis-centered,' that sex can be more leisurely than they imagined." Sexual excitement can continue long after the erect penis has left the scene. When her partner is loving, caressing and affectionate, a woman can go on and on in the pleasure of her orgasms.

A FIRST FOR PETE AND MARIAN

Marian first joined my Tuesday morning women's group at the urging of her sister, who had already been a member for several months. On many occasions over the years Marian had expressed to her sister the dissatisfaction she felt with her sexual relationship with Pete.

She blamed Pete because she rarely was able to have an orgasm.

Not only does he ejaculate too quickly—before I have a chance to come—but he turns over and starts snoring the minute he's finished. Once he's through, it's all over, whether I like it or not! Most of the time I'm just left there . . . hanging.

When Marian first learned from other women in the group that in the PLEASURE PROCESS their partners found it possible to repeatedly experience erection and orgasm during an evening of lovemaking, she was interested and intrigued—but skeptical:

I discovered very early in our marriage that Pete is just not one of those guys who can get it up a second time. I remember one night on our honeymoon, I felt so good I wanted to keep going after he came. I let Pete rest for a while, thinking he would get hard again—but he didn't. Then I did everything I could imagine to him, but nothing happened. Finally we both felt like failures. I was so exhausted I just gave up and we fell asleep.

This set the pattern for our sex life, because today, the minute he comes and gets soft, he quits. I feel cheated. I have come to resent the very sight of that soft, shriveled-up penis of his because I know he's been satisfied and I haven't.

In spite of her skepticism Marian continued attending the group. After weeks of listening to the other women share the positive results they were getting from practicing the PLEASURE PROCESS with their partners,

Marian became hopeful about what it could mean to her sex life with Pete. She couldn't wait to get home after group sessions to explain the steps and exercises to him. But when she told Pete what could be in store for *him*—as many as four or five erections when they practiced the steps—he was the one who became the skeptic:

> *Let's face it, Marian, four or five times a night is just locker-room hyperbole! I haven't heard that kind of bull since I was sixteen. And I knew better than to buy it then. I know you believe everything you hear in group, but you're going to have a hard time convincing me that you can reduce lovemaking to a mechanical, step-by-step procedure and get those kinds of results.*

Marian continued attending the women's group and continued practicing the PLEASURE PROCESS exercises when she was home alone. While she couldn't get Pete to do the steps with her, he did agree to cooperate by not limiting or interrupting her if she wanted to talk or share images during their sex. But he insisted that his participation would remain the same; he wasn't going to change the way he felt comfortable making love.

One night after sex, however, as Pete was just about to turn over, Marian asked him to keep hugging her. She was surprised when he did. He was affectionate and loving. He not only hugged her for a long time, but began gently rubbing her back, too. She could hardly believe what was happening. "Wow," she thought to herself, "at last he's actually doing the steps!"

Then Pete began playing with her vagina. He was hugging her from behind and she could feel his soft-on against the back of her thigh. It was the first time she had ever felt his soft penis against her body during sex.

She loved the sensation. As he continued to kiss the back of her neck and play with her, she became more and more aroused. Suddenly images began flashing into her mind. Without wondering if what she was "seeing" was appropriate, she said:

> *I'm wearing my little pink sunsuit. I can't be more than three or four years old. I'm sitting on my grandpa's lap, wiggling around. We're playing pat-a-cake and laughing. Even through his pants I can feel his soft-on against the back of my bare leg. It feels so good.*

As Marian talked about the pleasurable memory of her grandfather, she quickly transferred back to Pete. She began fondling his soft-on and asked him to get on top of her. Then she began rubbing it against her vagina and telling him how good his soft penis felt. She switched back and forth from her grandfather to Pete, explaining how wonderful their soft-ons felt to her.

Suddenly she was orgasming.

While watching Marian so completely immersed in her sexual feelings, Pete found himself becoming aroused, as well. He got so caught up in the excitement of listening to Marian's images and feeling her movements that before long he became erect again. This was a real surprise for both of them.

They had sex three times that evening . . . a first in their seven years of married life.

The Tide Will Return

Inexperienced lovers tend to stop lovemaking the moment ejaculation occurs. This is like leaving the banquet table before the main course has been served.

The happy experience of Pete and Marian was no accident. It is a common outcome for lovers who are learning to enjoy the romance of the soft-on. Men don't have to turn over and play "Hide and Go Sleep." Their soft-ons can become a delightful part of the erotic fun and play. They don't have to rationalize that once is enough because they're afraid they won't be able to "get it up" again. If a man wants more erections, he can have them; if you both want more orgasms, you can have them.

Too often the man feels ashamed of his soft-on and the woman feels afraid of it. He's concerned he won't be able to achieve another erection that night and she's convinced it's all her fault because she's not exciting enough for him.

Stop all this negative thinking.

The tide will return.

Instead of turning away . . . continue hugging.

Instead of being silent . . . share your feelings.

Instead of feeling inadequate . . . explore the sensuality of the soft-on.

Another erection will be coming along. It may take minutes or hours, but it doesn't matter, because during the PROCESS you will be sharing so much pleasure.

Keep the Woman Going

Once each of you accepts that the penis is sensual whether it's erect or not, there's more pleasure ahead for both of you.

When a man can better understand the female anatomy he will know that a good deal of sensory stimulation can occur just by taking the head of his soft penis and rubbing it against his partner's clitoris and the opening of her vagina. This can provide enough stimulation to this area to allow orgasm to occur for her.

At any point when the tide recedes and the man has a soft-on, he can maintain his partner's level of excitement in the *orgasmic continuum* by keeping her going. He can do this by using his soft-on or the rest of his body: his hands and mouth can stimulate her clitoris and nipples; his lips and tongue can enjoy the feeling of kissing her and being kissed.

It's important for him to contact as *many* of her erogenous zones as possible. For example, when one of his fingers is inside his lover's vagina, his thumb is on her clitoris, his other hand is fondling her breasts, and he's kissing her mouth—four erogenous areas are being stimulated simultaneously. The more areas he can touch on, the more orgasms she will experience.

One way to do this is by getting into what I call the "Bass Fiddle" position:

The man lies on his side, facing and holding his partner, who is on her back lying right next to him. Her hips are crossing over his hips, positioned so that she can feel his soft penis on the upper back side of her thighs, near her vagina. The upper part of his left arm is underneath her shoulders and the lower part of this arm comes around, leaving his left hand free to cover her breast. His right hand can then massage (and/or penetrate) her vagina, anus and clitoris. He plays her body as a musician would play a bass fiddle.

When you and your lover lie intertwined in this loving way, caressing and feeling so close, you will forget your negative conditioning, your guilts and fears. He will no longer be scrutinizing the turgidity/flaccidity of his penis . . . and neither will you. Instead you will be focusing in on the sensations of your body and the pleasurable feelings of his being so close. You will feel free to touch and enjoy your own skin, breasts, vagina and anus, while your hands are free to caress your partner's body.* You will both be discovering the enormous depths and range of sensuality that is available to you when you continue your love play beyond ejaculation.

Most people have so little appreciation of their sexual potential that they are quite content, and often delighted, to achieve a single orgasm and fall off to sleep. They have no idea that they have just barely uncovered the tip of the erotic iceberg. They don't realize that a mountain of sensuality lies waiting beneath.

When you can think of your sensuality as a continuum (ranging from, say, zero to 100) rather than as a finite point terminating at orgasm, you will better understand the principles underlying this PROCESS. When you consider that your first orgasm may only take you to point number 10 on this continuum, you realize that as much as 90 percent of your sensuality may as yet be untapped.

The tragedy of most sex is that it ends with the first orgasm. This tragedy is perpetuated by an almost universal lack of comprehension of the emotional and physiological capability of the human body. In the PLEASURE PROCESS, orgasm is just the beginning of your sensual voyage.

I want you to become aware of *your* capability. It isn't something you need to acquire . . . you came equipped with it at birth. As you continue to practice the steps of the PLEASURE PROCESS, you will automatically tap into *your* sensual reserves and develop and expand *your* sexuality.

---

* For at least ten minutes or more following ejaculation you can avoid touching his penis. Many men dislike having their penises touched immediately after ejaculation as they often feel tender.

The Pay-Off for Him

In the PLEASURE PROCESS there is a tremendous pay-off for the man. Formerly nonerogenous areas of his body begin to come alive as he experiences new erotic sensations during this post-ejaculatory period. The longer the lovemaking continues, the more sensual his entire body (not just his penis) will become.

Another pay-off is that he will discover in his partner a remarkably responsive woman whose willingness to experiment and explore will be contagious and exhilarating. He will have unleashed an erotic being whose enthusiasm for enjoying and pleasuring him sexually will be greater than he's ever known in her before.

During the *orgastic continuum* a new sexual atmosphere is created. Both partners share in the security of feeling successful and confident. There are no pressures about performing; it all just happens naturally, without worries, without fatigue. The healthy excitement of each partner reenergizes, refuels and recharges the other.

Most men physically require a resting (or refractory) period between erections. This period can be useful, an ideal time for a man to feel comfortable with his soft-on while putting the focus on enjoying his partner and keeping her going.

The soft-on is a part of the natural state of man. Most of the time during a man's normal day his penis is soft and he feels comfortable and relaxed about it. But during sexual play this natural state causes him to feel inadequate and anxious.

These feelings are encouraged by the women who typically fear and/or ignore the soft-on. But a flaccid penis is still an erogenous zone. Not only will your partner derive pleasure from having his soft-on played with, but you will also find it exciting once you learn to view his soft-on as a part of the lovemaking process, instead of as a symbol of failure for both of you.

You can rub it against your vagina, cradle it between your breasts, kiss, suck and caress it . . . be experimental and have fun! Play with it! Enjoy the soft-on—not for the purpose of making it hard again, but just for the pleasure of holding and fondling it in its soft state.

Between the contagion of your reveling in your *orgastic continuum* and your stimulating his soft penis, it is very unlikely that your partner's soft-on will remain soft! Many of my male patients who had never before had more than one orgasm during lovemaking report that because of what they have learned in the PLEASURE PROCESS, it is not unusual for them to have three to five orgasms. A man who typically becomes tired or loses interest in sex after one or two orgasms will find that he, much like his partner, will *want* to go on and on. His body will become capable of amazing sexual stamina and endurance.

In the PLEASURE PROCESS the man learns that his body, *in any state,* can be a source of joy for his partner and for himself; gone is the woman who resents and deprecates the soft-on; gone is the man who fears and hides it. Both partners accept, enjoy, and luxuriate in the natural ebb and flow of the loving experience.

Chapter 15

The Terror of Intimacy

How can I dare to love you completely, fully, totally? How can I dare to invest all of myself and risk being totally dependent on you? If you should die, what then? What will happen to me? How will I survive? How will I ever be able to walk straight again—to smile, to be gay, to hear laughter, to watch lovers walk hand in hand in the street?

Or if you should leave me by moving toward another woman—would that be worse than your dying? More difficult to bear? Would I be able to live through that?

I won't take a chance. I won't risk it.

I know what I'll do—

I won't get too close to you—too intimate.

I won't get too dependent on you.

I'll just play it cool.

I wonder deep down if being that vulnerable—if needing and depending on you so much—wouldn't be a kind of death in itself? Because if I should lose you, that would be it—then I'd be lost, too.

*   *   *

This is the unconscious voice of the fear of dependency. But it is rare that people can lay bare their fragile innards in so direct a manner. Most of us are too frightened even to acknowledge our own vulnerability and dependency, much less to express it openly. Yet underlying the defensive words that we do use is this hidden message: we long for intimacy. And ironically, without realizing it, we are active in preventing it.

The wonderful gift of the PLEASURE PROCESS is that it creates an opportunity for you and your lover to experience a new depth of intimacy and caring. But with this level of intimacy comes dependency, and therein lies the rub.

The Expectation of Loss

When we are able to be loving and giving of ourselves to another, a special bond of intimacy is established. At the beginning of a relationship this bond is fragile. It becomes strengthened over time by the adding on of the emotional closeness that comes with shared time, shared plans, shared happy and sad occasions, shared hopes.

This kind of intimacy can be tolerable and even comfortable for many couples, and can sometimes be sustained over long periods of time. But, it is when both *physical and emotional closeness* are achieved by the adding on of wonderful sex that fears of being vulnerable begin to tear at the bonding.

With exceptional closeness, lovers often become frightened and experience a sense of danger—of impending pain, abandonment or loss. When this happens they feel confused. It seems inappropriate that the threat of being hurt or left should appear at so happy and loving a time. But when you consider the way a normal child grows up, the fear of suffering some kind of loss after feeling close isn't very difficult to understand. Daily in many homes there are so many hurts, so much confusion and miscommunication, that even in the healthiest parent-child relationship the abandonment-following-intimacy configuration is present.

This occurs innocently. Can you remember how you felt when:

—after the closeness and intimacy of being nursed, your body melding into mother's, she put you back into your crib *and left you?*

—after the closeness and intimacy of being bathed and oiled by your mother's soothing hands, she laid you down for a nap *and left you?*

—after the closeness and intimacy of being powdered and diapered, kissed and cooed, mother set you in your playpen, gave you a toy, *and left you?*

—after the closeness and intimacy of sharing your first few years with mother, she marched you into the alien environment of a nursery school or kindergarten, introduced you to a group of strangers, *and left you?*

And so on. . . . As you grew up the abandonment continued, yet this was *normal* for her to do. She had other needs and demands on her time. And even if she didn't, it wouldn't have been healthy for her or for you if she had spent 24 hours a day catering to your needs.

A healthy and caring mother, during the course of her busy day, must frequently separate from her child. But from these constant separations the child often learns that intimacy is an ephemeral state.

Then there are the unhealthy homes where, unfortunately, the parents are so troubled themselves that very often they subject their children to treatment that is unreasonably cruel, rejecting and abandoning. For the children who are products of these painful beginnings, even the slightest show of intimacy is so rare, so unfamiliar, that it may be frightening and uncomfortable when it does occur.

To one degree or another, in a healthy, nurturing household or in a severely damaging one, we all learn to anticipate that abandonment will be close on the heels of intimacy. This expectation is so deeply ingrained that, long before anything disruptive has occurred or before any discernible cause can be found, partners start inching away from the closeness of their lovemaking and their tender embraces. They each begin to prepare themselves for the break they fear is imminent. They unconsciously structure a negative emotional climate to make their withdrawal justifiable. Much as a prizefighter prepares for a match by building up his muscles and stamina, lovers start to "build up" the grievances and irritations they'll need to use in order to distance and separate from each other.

Magnifying the Fear

The first two steps of the PLEASURE PROCESS were designed to help you deal with the fear of loss by abandonment and establish a new and safe bonding of emotional and physical (although nonsexual) closeness. Then, as the succeeding steps unfold, a warm environment of safety and mutual trust is created where you can learn to share more and approve of yourself. But it is when you go beyond this point—when you move from emotional into sexual closeness—that a new loss presents itself, a new threat appears. It is the fear of losing *ourselves*.

When the sex is deeply satisfying and the connection so complete, might we lose our body integrity into the oneness of the union? Will we be able to maintain and assert our individual personalities, values, prejudices, dreams and judgments? In good sex, and especially in the PLEASURE PROCESS, the blending becomes so close that emotional and physical differentiations become vague. As the lovemaking heightens, it is no longer "my" arms, "my" legs and "my" body. Rather the "me" becomes "us" and the "you" becomes "we." And as the pleasure crescendoes, your partner so identifies with the intensity of your feelings that "your" orgasms become "our" orgasms.

While this may sound like paradise —and it is—nonetheless this dissolution of boundaries poses a threat to self-definition. We unconsciously resist giving up the one thing we cherish as private and inviolate when we are children—our physical separateness.

We grow up accustomed to having our parents invade our thoughts, our plans, our actions—our worlds. It seems there is little left to us. They own everything . . . everything except our bodies. At least our bodies belong to us. Here our parents have *no* control. We get older, taller and our features change, in spite of the power they exercise over us. Our breasts develop, our hips broaden, we grow hair in special places, and these processes are all very private and precious to us. At last, we have something we can call our *own*. We can lay claim to a territory, a place to encase our secret thoughts, our fantasies and our dreams, a place belonging exclusively to us . . . our bodies.

When you consider the importance of the need to protect and define your physical boundaries, it is understandable how the quality of sex that you can experience in the PLEASURE PROCESS adds on to the ever-present fears you harbor of loss by abandonment or rejection.

It is no wonder that so many lovers unconsciously fear entrusting themselves to the arms of intimacy.

More Obstacles to Intimacy

In case, by some miracle of birth, you escaped all of the above problems and landed in an *ideal* home, with *ideal* parents, and enjoyed an *ideal* childhood (and I believe that none of this is possible), you still couldn't have avoided all the fears of closeness because of the environment in which we grow up.

There are certain cultural implants we learn as children which suggest that "after good must come bad." This notion is reinforced by our society, which continues to remind us throughout our lives that being happy or having fun may be taking a chance—it may be an invitation to danger. So whenever something wonderful happens, there is a fear that we may be tempting the gods.

Many rituals have evolved over the centuries to deal with this fear. In Mediterranean countries, for example, you can see old women spitting on the ground in an effort to appease the gods after something joyful has occurred. Even in our so-called modern technological society people are not immune to such superstitious beliefs and behaviors. Surely you can remember yourself or one of your friends knocking wood when someone has mentioned your good fortune.

The belief in these superstitious rituals, intended to ward off punishment anticipated as a consequence of pleasure, often carries over into sex. And in the PLEASURE PROCESS, where so many highs and sensual ecstasies are experienced, many people expect it is *inevitable* that some kind of pain or distancing must follow such joy.

After sex, most of us can endure our tender, intimate feelings for only a short time before we become anxious and want to separate. We unconsciously are concerned that the gods will descend in some form to punish us, so we stop the discomfort of waiting by finding a way to punish ourselves: we bring to an end the closeness. This is the predictable "pain state" most of us unwittingly set up to destroy our happiness when we become intimate.

Each of us goes about this destruction in our own way, rarely conscious of what we are doing or why. We feel compelled—almost driven—to unfold our particular style of pain or fighting soon after the sex stops. By fighting we take away our pleasure before it is taken from us. We engineer a thousand little separations in preparation for the finality of that omnipresent loss we fear by rejection, abandonment or death. We experience the pain of separation without having to wait for it, because it seems to hurt less when we can control the onset ourselves.

How We Do It: Fighting

One of the ways in which we bring on the emotional death of our intimacy is by fighting. The themes that surround our fights typically involve some form of resentment or blaming. We blame our partners, money problems, the children, in-laws—whatever will work at the moment to disrupt the loving flow. It can begin with a seemingly innocent comment, something we think would never bother our partner. And the fight that ensues is often a surprise to us.

Whichever vehicle we use to kill the good feelings, the result is the same: distance and emotional pain. Each family passes down from generation to generation its chant, a neurotic chorus it uses to destroy the joy of the moment. Without awareness we fall into it. First we're high and are feeling great . . . then . . . crash! We feel ourselves going down, down, down. Each partner is confused about how it all happened. Each one thinks it must have been the other's fault and is absolutely certain of his or her own innocence. Each may wonder why problems always seem to arise soon after periods of closeness.

Here are some examples of the sorts of subtle jabs and needlings that can ignite the conflict. Do you recognize *your* (or your partner's) personal style in any of these? While still lying in each other's arms after sex, have you ever said or heard:

—"I don't want to hurt your feelings, love, *but* you almost turned me off, you were moaning and groaning so loud . . ."

—"I hate to bring this up now, dear, *but* my mother really felt insulted when you . . ."

—"Honey, I don't want to upset you at a time like this, *but* I got an estimate on the dent you put in my car, and . . ."

—"I've been afraid to tell you what your son did at school today, dear, *but* I feel you've got to know, and . . ."

Why the Fighting Works

Fighting reduces the terror of dependency. It offers us a sense, however negative, of our territory and space, of being separate. In good sex we're so joined, territories become blurred. We tend to get lost into each other.

While this is the state of nirvana that people say they seek, few of us can cope with it. Closeness creates so much anxiety that we think, "If anything bad happens, how am I going to live without this person? How can I tolerate all this dependency? There's no room here just for *me*."

When the fight comes after sex, we feel relieved. "Whew! I'm *not* dependent. I made it. I'm safe now."

The reason that we unconsciously start these fights, and impose distance and conflict when we're feeling intimate, is because we know how to deal in this way. We have had plenty of experience with disharmony during childhood; we're old hands at it. Though we talk a lot about wanting more joy and happiness in our lives, when we are faced with pleasure for an extended period of time we become *un*comfortable.

Fighting may be painful, but we feel safer in the throes of an argument; it's something we know how to do. Most people tend to choose the familiar over the unknown because new experiences seem threatening. We know how to survive with loneliness and distance. We fear that trying something new may lead to strange and ominous consequences. We don't want to chance it.

We'd rather go back to what we're used to doing . . . feeling lonely and distant. It may be unrewarding, but at least we have the skills to deal with it, and, best of all, we *know what to expect.*

How We Do It: Negative Dampeners

It may be hard to understand why so many people have difficulty enjoying the good fortune and happy events that come into our lives. We all tend to believe that we *can* handle success when it comes, that we *can* handle wealth, happiness and unending pleasure. But very few of us can. For most of us, handling joy is difficult.

Parents, in their efforts to protect their offspring from possible letdowns or failures, build negative cautions into their children's expectations.

Often, if a child sounds very happy, positive, or confident, a concerned parent will fear for the child's later disappointments and attempt to cushion the blow. For example, a little girl comes home from school jubilant and exclaims, "Boy, Mom, I'm the *best* speller in the *whole* class. I got every word right today." The mother, fearing her daughter will become discouraged if she doesn't do that well next time, throws in a negative dampener by saying, "Now, honey, don't get too cocky. No one likes a showoff."

Or take the example of the teenage girl who returns home from her first date with a new boy. She runs up to her father beaming, "Oh, gosh, Dad! I had such a great time. Didn't you think he was super?" The father, hoping to spare his daughter the possibility of a broken heart in case the boy doesn't share her enthusiasm, throws in a negative dampener with this caution: "Don't get so excited. You just met him. He may not prove to be so 'super' when you get to know him better."

When a child's feelings of happiness and elation are consistently followed by a parent's well-intentioned put-downs and discouragements, it isn't long before a firm association is established and the damaging connection is again made:

After good, be prepared for bad.

After years of this kind of training and repetition, eventually we take over our parents' role and deliver the negative dampeners to ourselves. In situations where we feel especially happy or joyous, we become anxious and fearful of impending doom.

By the time we grow into adulthood, this negative association of "bad following good" is so deeply embedded in our subconscious that rather than allow the doom to hang over and threaten us, we throw it in our faces. Then we don't have to wait and wonder when it's going to happen. We get it over with.

It is especially common to do this after having good sex. When you can abandon yourself in sex, feeling so happy and so close, when there is so much joy, there is a fear of overdosing with happiness. Besides, you think, you don't deserve that much pleasure. This is when you start manufacturing the negative dampeners, the blaming, and the fighting. Your childhood training and social conditioning don't permit you to tolerate that much fun and freedom.

When sex is extremely passionate and fulfilling, you're afraid that what happened was a one-time accident or a miracle. It was *too* good. Then you start worrying: what are you going to do for an encore? You'd better quit while you're ahead. You don't want to become dependent upon another person for all that joy. You're so convinced you'll never be able to feel that much again, you don't even want to try, because this time you might fail. You don't want to become that vulnerable. It is too big a risk to take.

What will happen if your partner leaves you? You didn't have to worry earlier, because it didn't mean as much to you; you never got that close before. Besides, you didn't know *how good it could get*. Now that you do, the loss could be overwhelming. If your partner leaves, you will feel wiped out. You think it's safer when you don't care that deeply. That's why you look for a way to separate and stop the loving.

Preventing Intimacy

An alternative to stopping the pleasure that could accompany intimacy is to prevent any possibility of intimacy in the first place. Most people are very inventive in their ability to reduce pleasure. They find many ways to go about killing the joy of being intimate. Do you see yourself in any of these examples?

1. Self-Criticism

Self-criticism is a handy tool to bring you down and put an end to your good feelings and your motivation to improve your life. You can do this by criticizing your appearance, your ideas and judgments, and your behavior. The saboteur in you may use criticism to try to discourage you. Negative comparisons like these will work:

> *"I'll bet that everyone reading this book is sailing through the steps and doing great . . . everyone except my husband and me. I'll never make it to dozens of orgasms. We can't even get beyond Step II. I know it's all my fault. I may as well quit now."*

STOP your destructive comparisons. Don't do this to yourself. It is rare for anyone to "sail through" the learning of a new experience. Some of the couples I've worked with have spent weeks on a single step. Recognize that your self-criticism is just another defensive device you may unconsciously be employing to protect you from experiencing change and fully expressing the vast range of your sensuality.

TERROR OF INTIMACY 249

Move at your own pace, at whatever rate is comfortable for both of you. Don't look for perfection in your body, mind or spirit. There isn't any. Just keep practicing, and you'll find the steps *will* work for you.

2. Not Being "in the Mood"

While we have discussed this in Chapter 6, "Prelude to the Process," I bring it up here because I want you to recognize that, while not being in the mood for sex can be entirely legitimate, it is too often a smoke screen—an expression of the terror and anxiety that intimacy and closeness can create.

Not being "in the mood" frequently extends to physical symptoms which also stop the closeness and serve to ensure that no intimacy will be achieved. The complaints most commonly listed by patients include vaginal disorders like herpes, trichomonas and yeast infections, and bladder infections such as cystitis. Headaches, backaches, fatigue, colds and flu are also high on the list.

It is interesting to note that among the women I've worked with, certain of them—the personalities who tend to be more aggressive sexually and who rarely are not "in the mood"—seldom contract vaginal disorders.

The body and the mind are so inextricably linked that there is a close connection between physical illness and emotional needs. While the entire process is highly unconscious, among the couples I've treated who are the most frightened of intimacy and dependency, one of the partners will almost invariably develop a physical problem. This effectively serves to prohibit sexual relations between them. Psychosomatic illnesses, then, become the solutions they use to prevent intimacy.

MICHAEL AND SUE

One such couple came in to see me not long ago. Michael's complaint was that sex had become so infrequent for them that they rarely made love more than once every two months. Sue's complaint was that she *had* to avoid intercourse because of a painful burning sensation in her vagina.

I instructed them that for one week they were to hug every night for 10 minutes before going to sleep. I emphasized that under *no* circumstances were they to engage in intercourse. I received a commitment from each of them to follow these rules.

At our next session Sue reported that for the first time in many years the burning sensation had disappeared.

———

If you have problems of infrequently being "in the mood," or if you suspect that the vaginal disorders or other psychosomatic complaints that you are sometimes troubled by have deeper significance, I want you to know that the PLEASURE PROCESS is designed to help you. You *can* get over these hindrances—these physical and/or emotional barriers that prevent you from happy sexual loving and sharing.

3. There's Too Little Energy Left

There are numerous behavioral patterns which you can use to keep yourself physically exhausted and emotionally preoccupied, so that there will be *too little energy left* for intimacy and sex. Workaholics, alcoholics, "drug"-aholics, "food"-aholics and "hygiene"-aholics are among the people that fit into this category.

Keeping yourself exhausted can take on many forms: the career workaholic, whether male or female, does this by starting work too early, staying too late, and feeling totally spent at the end of the day. He or she has *too little physical or emotional energy left* for anything, let alone the time for intimacy and intercourse.

The homemaker can be a combination workaholic/ hygiene-aholic. She can keep herself exhausted by meticulously scouring and polishing every surface, zealously guarding or cleaning up the children every minute, serving gourmet meals, or all of the above. She depletes her energy reserves by working all day and half the night and has *too little left* for lovemaking.

It can be, and is, healthy to get involved with your work, home life, and family. But when the devotion is at the expense of enjoying other important aspects of your life (e.g., sex), then this devotion may approach fanaticism, compulsion, martyrdom and sacrifice . . . all of which are *un*healthy.

The alcoholics, drug-aholics and food-aholics are a group which I like to separate into a special package. Their addictions have a built-in "double whammy." Not only is the cost in time and energy of their addictive problems great, but the physical ramifications that result from their food, chemical or alcohol abuse further complicate their lives. It's much like taking on an additional full-time job. They must have the energy required to meet the demands of normal living and still be able to muster the energy needed to satisfy the expense in time and pain of their addictions.

These compulsions can serve many other destructive purposes: they keep us from feeling adequate, appreciated and worthy. But even more, they serve as a defense against the terror of closeness and intimacy. Are you using some kind of compulsion to protect yourself from the vulnerability of intimacy?

4. The "Five-Minutes-to-Eight" Syndrome

Do you or your husband find yourselves becoming sexually aroused at five minutes to eight, when you know your guests will be arriving at eight? This could be just another smoke screen, a way to avoid the terror of intimacy without letting yourself look at the underlying causes.

You certainly can have a fun "quickie" in a few minutes, but when your standard operating procedure is to allot yourselves so little time to make love, this promises to reduce the intimacy of the loving experience.

5. Only When It's Impossible

An offshoot of the "five-minutes-to-eight" syndrome is the "only-when-it's-impossible" routine. My hunch is that this gambit *isn't* foreign to you. It happens when your mate chooses to fondle your breasts and passionately kiss your ears and neck when:

—you're standing at the kitchen sink, elbow-deep in soapsuds;
—you've just begun to nurse your hungry baby;
—you're having a serious telephone conversation with a close friend who is in trouble;
—you're feeling panicky, rushing to create that gourmet meal for his boss.

Do you recognize your lover's behavior in any of these examples? If so, you may be thinking to yourself now, "Oh! No wonder he's always doing these things to me. It's really because he's afraid to get close."

You're right . . . but there's another important ingredient to consider.

Equal Emotional Partners

Before you get too excited about your newfound insight into your *partner's* problems with intimacy, it's important now that we take a look at *you.* Psychologically speaking, *equal* emotional partners find each other.

Let me explain. Say I invented a "Sexual Intimacy Scale" which ranged from 1 to 10 and which accurately measured an individual's ability to have sexual-sensual closeness and intimacy. And let us say that you registered 5.8 on that scale. If this were the case, you would unconsciously select a love partner who *also* measured 5.8 on that same scale. Overtly it might *appear* that one of you was a frigid 2.2 and the other an ever-ready 9.9, but even when one of the partners claims to want sex all the time and the other seems uninterested, don't be fooled. No matter how much your overt behaviors might contradict the reality of your "sameness," psychologically we each find and pair up with our precise emotional equals. Otherwise the chemistry wouldn't work in the first place and the relationship couldn't get off the ground.

Even before you met each other, your intimacy/distancing ratio was established. Both of you came into the relationship capable of achieving a *specific amount* of closeness and intimacy. This amount was originally determined during the course of your first important relationship—the one you experienced as an infant with your parents. The quality and intensity of intimacy and closeness you were allowed to exchange with them was well demonstrated by the time you were four years old.

So now, though you may think it is your partner who is responsible for stopping the pleasure—or it is your partner who is to blame for starting all those fights— in a relationship it takes the interaction of *both* partners to set up the distancing and pain.

Even though your sexual personalities may express themselves through highly different behavioral patterns, in truth they are deep-rooted mirror images of each other. In fact, your psychological fittings are so closely matched to his that if he's distancing and preventing the closeness, I want you to stop and question if *you* are too!

Since this may be difficult to understand, here are some examples to consider. While they may or may not reflect your particular style of avoiding closeness, they may enable you to start thinking about the particular methods that you *do* use to prevent sexual intimacy:

—Do you manage to start talking about serious problems as you're getting ready for bed, ensuring that you'll both be too upset to make love?

—Do you object to putting a lock on your bedroom door because you're worried that your children will feel left out if they can't freely roam in and out of your room?

—Do you refuse to take the phone off the hook during lovemaking because you don't want to miss that "emergency" call?

—Do you encourage friends to drop by any time they like, making certain that one day you'll be interrupted during sex?

—Do you insist on allowing your small children to crawl into bed between you when they wake up at night, rationalizing that this is the best way to help them feel cozy and safe?

—Do you hate putting in your diaphragm, insist you'll gain weight with the pill, or fear the IUD will cause cancer, thus causing the possibility of pregnancy to limit the frequency of your sexual encounters?

—Are you still living with mother, arguing that it's the only way to save money, while your husband has difficulty erecting because of the proximity of her bedroom to yours?

—Do you suffer from the "Statue-of-Liberty" complex and feel compelled to take in stray relatives and friends, reducing your privacy and the opportunities to have sex?

Whatever style *you* use to create distance, it isn't likely that you are consciously aware of what you are doing; you inherited your style so long ago that it is second nature to you now. The behaviors themselves are so subtle, so indirect and so much a part of your habitual repertoire, that unless someone outside of your family helped to make you aware, you would find it almost impossible to detect them.

Take a moment now to look back to your childhood. Can you remember seeing your mother and father openly expressing affection and warmth with each other, caressing and embracing each other at frequent intervals? Or did they consider it improper or embarrassing to display affection in front of you? Or, even worse, did you grow up in a household devoid of any show of intimacy or closeness because of an ongoing war between your parents?

If you're like most people, there was little or no sensuality, affection or closeness for you to observe as a child. So how could you have learned the language of intimacy when you never heard even a word of it uttered?

You couldn't. But you can start learning it *right now*.

Steps Toward Change

By first *seeing* that you are 50-percent responsible for the lack of intimacy in your life, you can change. You can learn to exceed the limited bounds of closeness that were defined for you when you were small.

Step One in changing is *seeing* how you are preventing the intimacy. Step Two is being *warm* and *accepting* of yourself when you can finally see what you are doing. Step Three is *understanding*. You will be kinder to yourself when you understand that your distancing was learned. You are modeling the behavioral patterns that you became familiar with as a child.

By *warmly accepting* yourself, you can start communicating to your partner bits of information about your childhood history and what you learned, or didn't learn, about intimacy. And if you want him to follow suit, be careful to avoid delivering any judgments, criticism or blame. Then you both will feel safe, and a loving camaraderie will develop as you share painful and confusing childhood memories that reveal the similarity of your emotional histories.

You're both in the same boat; that's why you're together. And together you have an *even better* chance to change. Because while we're often blind to our own shortcomings, we seldom overlook the flaws of our partners. Or, in more psychological terms, while it may sometimes be difficult for either of you to recognize your *own* unconscious avoidance behaviors, each of you will be able to clearly spot the resistance of the other. And that's how you can help yourselves: by each alerting the other, *gently and warmly*, when the distancing starts. I emphasize "gently and warmly" because if there is the slightest smell of criticism or blaming, your progress will stop.

And don't get discouraged if the changing is slow. After all, old tapes take priority over new ones; they've been part of your life longer. Just get back to your homework and exercises whenever you can, and be warm and accepting of yourself and him when you see the excuses and avoidance coming. Your new tapes will gain in strength and your feelings of safety and comfort will increase each time you practice the steps of the PLEASURE PROCESS.

Stopping the Saboteur

Watch out for the saboteur in you. Watch out for the *new* excuses you'll both be inventing to stop the intimacy and move away from practicing the steps. Because once the pleasure that comes with the PROCESS starts flowing, there's a tendency to become frightened and pull away.

When you *see* this happening, this is your signal for action. Say to yourself, "I'm dredging up the old tapes and playing out the distancing I learned as a child. And I'm going to try to stop, now. I deserve this pleasure."

Now you're *seeing* your terror of intimacy. Good . . . that's Step One. Next, remember that Step Two is being *warm* and *accepting* of yourself (and your partner), and that the important third step is to *understand* that you're doing this because there is a tremendous emotional pull to replicate the familiar, early conditions of our childhoods.

When you can create an atmosphere of warmth and understanding, you and your partner will begin to express your *real* fears—not the camouflage of excuses, blaming and fighting that you've been using to create the distance and tear away your blanket of closeness.

Take a Chance Today

My hope is that by understanding your early beginnings, your fears of abandonment and rejection, and your difficulty in establishing and maintaining a loving relationship, you'll be better able to set aside your fears about intimacy and take a chance today.

Risk trusting yourself in the arms of your lover.

Risk changing the negative tapes of your childhood history.

Risk the true pleasure of omnisensuality.

I want you to go back and invite your precious erotic child to roam free—to be spontaneous—to come out to play and dance with you in your bed.

I want you to be able to open the door and uncover the magic of your beautiful hidden room.

I want you to know the fun of laughing and openly communicating during sex.

I want you to trust your images and give them safe passage to float from your thoughts to your lips, bringing with them all the passions and buried sensuality of your childhood.

I want you to know I'm proud that you were willing to take my hand. I've been happy sharing these hours with you. Yet, I'm sad because our work together is finished. But my words will be your friend, your guide, as you continue practicing the steps over and over again with your mate and by yourself.

The path to sensual intimacy and happiness has been marked off for you in the PLEASURE PROCESS, but the real key lies in *your* hands. Be your own source of wisdom, acceptance and approval. Believe in your goodness and kindness, in the innocence of your childhood. Then you will be able to go back and recapture the richness and originality of your unique self.

Goodbyes have always been difficult for me, and leaving is painful. But I feel good knowing you've read my words and trusted me. And now, you can trust *you*.

It's time now to close my book and open yourself up to feeling beautiful.

It's time now to let go of my hand.

It's time now to unleash the stunning power and purity of your own sensuality . . . the sensuality of *nice girls who do!*

Notes

1. These phrases may be attributed, in order, to the following gentlemen: Robert Burns, James Thurber and E. B. White, George Chapman, Addison, Ovid, Shakespeare, and Lord Byron.

2. Therese Benedek, "Discussion of Sherfey's Paper on Female Sexuality," *Journal of the American Psychoanalytic Association* 16 (1968), p. 446.

3. Joseph and Lois Bird, *Sexual Loving: The Experience of Love* (Garden City, New York: Doubleday & Company, 1976), p. 116.

4. Alexander Lowen, *Bioenergetics* (New York: Coward, McCann & Geoghegan, 1975), p. 245.

5. Andrew M. Barclay, "Sexual Fantasies in Men and Women," *Medical Aspects of Human Sexuality* 7:5 (May 1973), p. 212.

6. Molly Haskell, "The 2,000-Year-Old Misunderstanding: Rape Fantasy," *Ms.* (November 1976), p. 92.

7. E. Barbara Hariton, "The Sexual Fantasies of Women," *Psychology Today* (March 1973), p. 39.

8. Robert Latou Dickinson and Lura Beam, *A Thousand Marriages: A Medical Study of Sex Adjustment* (Baltimore: The Williams & Wilkins Company, 1931), p. 64.

9. Mathilda von Kemnitz, *The Triumph of the Will*, 1932.

10. Joseph and Lois Bird, *Sexual Loving*, p. 74.

11. A. C. Kinsey, W. B. Pomeroy, C. E. Martin, and P. H. Gebhard, *Sexual Behavior in the Human Female* (Philadelphia: Saunders, 1953), pp. 104–105.

12. "Quiz: Adolescent Sexuality," *Medical Aspects of Human Sexuality* 8:11 (November 1974), p. 79.

13. John Money, *Love and Love Sickness: The Science of Sex Gender Differences and Pair Bonding* (Baltimore: Johns Hopkins University Press, 1980).

14. Joseph and Lois Bird, *Sexual Loving*, p. 75.

15. Ashley Montagu, *Touching: The Human Significance of the Skin*, 2d ed. (New York: Harper & Row, Publishers, 1978), p. 4.

16. Raymond Babineau, M.D., and Allan J. Schwartz, Ph.D., "Reciprocity of Sexual Excitement," *Medical Aspects of Human Sexuality* 10:7 (July 1976), p. 132.

17. Alexander Lowen, *Bioenergetics*, p. 245.

18. William H. Masters and Virginia E. Johnson, *Human Sexual Response* (Boston: Little, Brown and Company, 1966), p. 131.

19. Mary Jane Sherfey, "The Evolution and Nature of Female Sexuality in Relation to Psychoanalytic Theory," *Journal of the American Psychoanalytic Association* 14 (1966), p. 99.

20. Lonnie Garfield Barbach, *For Yourself: The Fulfillment of Female Sexuality* (Garden City, New York: Doubleday & Company, 1975), p. xv.

21. Mary Jane Sherfey, "Evolution and Nature of Female Sexuality," p. 99.

22. Joseph and Lois Bird, *Sexual Loving*, p. 75.

Bibliography

Babineau, Raymond, M.D., and Schwartz, Allan J., Ph.D. "Reciprocity of Sexual Excitement." *Medical Aspects of Human Sexuality* 10:7 (July 1976).

Bakwin, Harry, M.D. "Erotic Feelings in Infants and Young Children." *Medical Aspects of Human Sexuality* (October 1974).

Barbach, Lonnie Garfield. *For Yourself: The Fulfillment of Female Sexuality.* Garden City, New York: Doubleday & Company, 1975.

Barclay, Andrew M. "Sexual Fantasies in Men and Women." *Medical Aspects of Human Sexuality* 7:5 (May 1973).

Benedek, Therese. "Discussion of Sherfey's Paper on Female Sexuality." *Journal of the American Psychoanalytic Association* 16 (1968).

Bird, Joseph and Lois. *Sexual Loving: The Experience of Love.* Garden City, New York: Doubleday & Company, 1976.

Butterfield, Oliver M. *Sexual Harmony in Marriage.* New York: Emerson, 1964.

Calderone, Mary Steichen, M.D., and Goldman, Phyllis and Robert P. *Release from Sexual Tensions.* New York: Random House, 1964.

Comfort, Alex. *More Joy.* New York: Crown Publishers, 1973.

Dickinson, Robert Latou, and Beam, Lura. *A Thousand Marriages: A Medical Study of Sex Adjustment.* Baltimore: The Williams & Wilkins Company, 1931.

Ellis, Albert, Ph.D., and Harper, Robert A., Ph.D. *The Marriage Bed.* New York: Tower, 1961.

Freud, Sigmund, M.D. *The Complete Psychological Works of Freud.* London: Hogarth Press, 1955.

Gould, Lois. "Pornography for Women." *New York Times Magazine,* 2 March 1975.

Hariton, E. Barbara. "The Sexual Fantasies of Women." *Psychology Today,* March 1973.

Haskell, Molly. "The 2,000-Year-Old Misunderstanding: Rape Fantasy." *Ms.,* November 1976.

Hawkins, David R. "Disturbing Erotic Fantasies." *Medical Aspects of Human Sexuality,* September 1974.

Hollender, Marc H. "Women's Coital Fantasies." *Medical Aspects of Human Sexuality,* 4 (1970).

Kaplan, Helen Singer. "Friction and Fantasy: No-Nonsense Therapy of Six Sexual Malfunctions." *Psychology Today,* October 1974.

Kardener, Sheldon H. "Rape Fantasies." *Journal of Health and Religion* 14:1 (1975).

Kegel, Arnold H., M.D. "Sexual Functions of the Pubococcygeus Muscle." *Western Journal of Surgery, Obstetrics and Gynecology* 60:10 (October 1952).

Kinsey, A. C.; Pomeroy, W. B.; Martin, C. E.; and Gebhard, P. H. *Sexual Behavior in the Human Female.* Philadelphia: Saunders, 1953.

Lowen, Alexander. *Bioenergetics.* New York: Coward, McCann & Geoghegan, 1975.

Marmor, Judd, M.D. "Some Considerations Concerning Orgasm in the Female." *Psychosomatic Medicine* 16:3 (May-June 1954).

Masters, William H. and Johnson, Virginia E. *Human Sexual Response.* Boston: Little, Brown and Company, 1966.

Money, John. *Love and Love Sickness: The Science of Sex Gender Differences and Pair Bonding.* Baltimore: John Hopkins University Press, 1980.

Money, John. "The Erotic Allure of the Breast." *Harper's Bazaar,* September 1976.

Money, John, and Tucker, Patricia. *Sexual Signatures: On Being a Man or a Woman.* Boston: Little, Brown & Company, 1975.

Montagu, Ashley. *Touching: The Human Significance of the Skin.* Second Edition. New York: Harper & Row, Publishers, 1978.

"Preparation for Parenthood." The American National Red Cross Manual Instructor's Guide, 1976.

"Quiz: Adolescent Sexuality." *Medical Aspects of Human Sexuality* 8:11 (November 1974).

Rainwater, Lee. "Some Aspects of Lower Class Sexual Behavior." *The Journal of Social Issues* 22:2 (April 1966).

Rice, Dabney. "The Indignity of Obligatory Coitus." *Harper's Bazaar,* November 1976.

Rosenberg, Jack Lee, *Total Orgasm.* New York: Random House, 1973.

Sherfey, Mary Jane. "The Evolution and Nature of Female Sexuality in Relation to Psychoanalytic Theory." *Journal of the American Psychoanalytic Association* 14 (1966).

ABOUT THE AUTHOR

Dr. Irene Kassorla is a practicing psychologist whose enormously successful breakthroughs in the field of sex therapy have brought her international fame.

Her academic credentials include B.A. and M.A. degrees in psychology from U.C.L.A. and a Ph.D. from the University of London's Institute of Psychiatry.

Dr. Kassorla has received many honors and awards, and has lectured and practiced throughout the Far East, South America, the Middle East, Europe and Australia. She is also the author of numerous scholarly papers on her work with autistic children.

Dr. Kassorla is equally famous as a television personality. Presently she lives in Los Angeles where she is well known for her lecture and television appearances.